The Condensed Book of Internet Marketing

Rick Kelly

The Condensed Book of Internet Marketing

Table of Contents

Introduction

Don't let anyone tell you that you can't produce an Internet marketing campaign *on your own*.

Take charge of your Internet marketing campaign, because an engaging and interesting business is just that: it's both fascinating and profitable. There aren't any shortcuts on the Internet; there is just the alluring combination of hard work, knowledge, technology, and a few more added ingredients – ingenuity and business.

As the Internet continues to grow, the possibilities for niche marketing continue to present themselves in new, different, and exciting ways. This is because new technology provides many new ways to contact and appeal to the people who buy. It's exhilarating to imagine the possibilities for communication with customers and ultimately, the increase in sales.

The reality, however, can be very different. Whether you are new to Internet marketing, or just under the gun to produce some sales, you may not find much help on the one place where there is so much free information – the Internet itself.

The challenge with the Internet is that like you, everyone else is also selling something as well. This makes it difficult to separate real and useful marketing information from a sales pitch for new products. Even if a website offers free marketing information, you may not get much out of it. What initially looks like instruction is really just a keyword-stuffed sales pitch for marketing software. This is advertising, and there is no shortage of it, or product information on the Internet.

Why are you confused About Internet Marketing?

It's because of the name droppers. These are the websites that are so full of product names that no one who isn't a tech geek could possibly sort them out. If you think you because you are new to the Internet that you can't keep up with technology, then you are looking at too many product-selling websites with links to other product-selling web sites to figure it out.

Think about what you have been sold so far including services, equipment, software, etc. Then think how about how much of it has produced sales. You may be happy, perplexed, or out of a lot of money.

The best way to tackle Internet Marketing is to understand the principles of marketing itself; and then get the technology that makes sense for your situation. This will be a unique combination that works for you to make sales.

Here are some things to think about:

- What product or message am I trying to sell?
- Who am I trying to reach?
- Where can I find my niche market?
- Why is my product different?
- How much should it cost?
- Who in my niche market is willing to buy it?
- Who else sells my product?
- What is the difference between me and them?
- Can we work together to reach a wider audience?
- What specific technology do I need to make sales?
- How do I keep up with new information?
- How do I narrow down my technology so that it doesn't take over my business?

These are all questions that you should be able to answer in order to have a successful Internet Marketing Campaign. The chapters in this book are divided up so that that all of the answers are broken down in an easy and informative way so that you can answer all of these questions.

Chapter One

Internet marketing is about reaching the *right people*.

The Differences between Marketing, Advertising, and Public Relations:

If you want to sell a product or get a message out on the Internet without spending a lot of money, it is important to understand the differences between marketing, advertising and public relations. This means knowing that spending money on advertising won't help sell a product if you don't have a solid, bona-fide marketing plan in place.

While advertising can create awareness for a product or solidify someone's perception of a brand, you cannot rely on paid advertising alone to create sales for your product. When you compare marketing and public relations to advertising, you'll realize why this is true. You will also save a lot in advertising dollars and prevent the misdirected energy that goes into unconnected advertising.

If you keep marketing as your number one goal, you can create an entire system of information that will lead to sales that are dependable. Organizing information about customers is what will actually increase sales and also builds relationships that are lasting. Recognizing the difference between advertising, marketing and public relations is the first step to increasing sales. The way to get started is to break everything down so it makes sense.

Here is a basic formula that you should always remember:

Advertising = Media
Marketing = Sales
Public Relations = News

These three equations make up the foundation of productive Internet marketing. By learning to appreciate the differences, you will stop wasting time and money feeding your anxieties, and instead, start producing sales.

Think about it this way. If you notice, when you talk about advertising for your product, you talk about the medium itself. This includes the colors in an ad, the size, where it's placed, and how much it costs. Then, if you talk to someone about sales figures and quarterly reports, you're talking to them about marketing. PR is usually something about your company that you hope is (or isn't) published in the news.

Don't Fall in Love with Advertising

Let's start with advertising, because it is the most popular way to establish anyone's identity. Advertising, quite literally, is the typography, fonts, logos, photography, art work, video, audio, music, jingles, slogans, copywriting, scripts, and other artistic elements that make up an advertisement. That's it - and no matter how incredible advertising is and how entertaining is, advertising is an unpredictable medium. In fact, the erratic nature of advertising can either make someone a fortune, or bankrupt and even discredit them.

The predictability of advertising falls apart even more in the distribution. This is because an advertising campaign will take all of the creative elements that are chosen and then distribute them through any kind of media available. This includes television, film, radio, the Internet, magazines, newspapers, flyers, inserts, billboards, direct mail, email, websites, and anywhere else that the advertiser can afford.

The results can be dramatic, but dramatic may not be what you are looking for if your advertisements are annoying. On the Internet, this can mean pop-up ads, banner ads, too many ads on websites, slow downloading ads, adult content ads, and ads that trick you into clicking on them in order to do something like change your browser. Throw in television ads, billboards and the radio, and viewers eventually wish that there was no such thing as advertising, and for that matter, the products associated with it.

It's our own fault. As a culture, we are so acclimated to advertising that we accept it as part of our daily lives. So we deal with it as a constant. We block it out, we absolutely hate it, or sometimes we enjoy it so much that we blog about it. We are so familiar with scheduled advertising, that it regulates our lives. It started with using the bathroom during a commercial on television and then evolved to blocking out pop-up ads while waiting for a download.

Advertising is also harmless, in the fact that we know it's there if we want it; and we know that we can turn it off if we don't. This love/hate relationship is wonderful for the casual consumer; but it's not so great for a business that has a deadline to generate sales.

If you've ever desperately needed some quick sales to generate income and tried to get them through advertising, you know the sinking feeling of a champion that has turned on you. The winning campaign that worked so well the first time has now miserably failed. No one can explain it; they just know when to move on to the next sure thing.

There is nothing like taking the last of your sales budget and spending it on some advertising and then waiting for something – or anything, to happen. To add insult to injury, advertising on the downside usually involves offering some type of crazy discount. This is the last thing a company can afford to give, but they can't afford not to do it. So when no one responds to advertising, it can be devastating both financially and emotionally.

You can ask yourself what you did wrong, but advertising won't answer you back. Believe what you want to justify the results of advertising, but there just aren't any direct connections that you can draw between advertising and sales except that sometimes the color red makes people hungry. While it's true that Internet advertising can be proven to increase traffic to your website or your brick and mortar store, it can't guarantee that anyone will buy anything once they get there.

This is because love it or hate it, we tune Internet advertising out unless it peaks our curiosity enough to click on an advertisement. Usually, that's just to see what it is about - especially if it has a well-written teaser that we can't resist. But as lovers of advertising, once our curiosity is satisfied, we go back to hating it. Pay-per-click advertising lulls everyone into a false sense of productivity. It gives the advertiser a feeling of cause to action, but turns out to be only a minor annoyance to the viewer.

However, when you are desperate for sales, that false sense of hope can set off a kind of dread that never goes away. This is the kind of feeling that Internet advertising execs prey on when you are at your weakest.

You ask yourself, what if that if the ad was cleverer or placed in a better position on the Internet? Or what if there were more ads, would it generate more sales? Internet advertising salespeople capitalize on this false sense of hope with the rationale that as an advertiser, you will only pay when people click on the advertisement. That's not a comforting thought for anyone who has to pin their hopes on advertising for sales revenue.

Marketing Generates Sales

While Internet advertising has its place, it is no substitute for a solid Internet marketing plan because advertising does not equal sales. In actuality, the definition of marketing *is* sales, and while advertising can be used along with sales, it is not at all the same. Always remember, advertising is basically all of the mediums used to communicate a message, and marketing is the means used to generate a sale.

This can be through verbal or written communication, or through a sales mechanism, like a web site. Internet marketing is the sum total of all your efforts to make a sale: including your product or service, a well-designed and easy to navigate website or e-commerce store, a sales pitch, any product information offered to the consumer, the price or fee you charge, the methods of payments, coupons that you accept, special promotions and offers, customer service, how the goods are delivered or services are supplied, warranties, return policies, and service agreements.

In essence, anything that you do to make a sale is marketing. As you can see, marketing has little or nothing to with advertising, and yet the two or always lumped together. However, the big difference between advertising and marketing is that marketing can be measured.

Internet advertising advocates always make attempts at measuring the results of advertising. For example, you will often find a box to fill out on most web sites asking 'How did you hear about us' when you purchase something or ask to be put on a mailing list. This kind of tracking is sketchy at best, and generally used by someone who wants everyone to believe that Internet advertising without marketing works.

Even if only a handful of customers express that they found the website through a banner ad that seems to be enough to justify dumping more money into advertising. Be forewarned: if you have to rely on nonscientific exit surveys to improve your product or your sales, you need to get back to marketing basics.

Of course, marketing – including product development and customer service- isn't as glamorous as the world of advertising and requires a lot more work, as well as the understanding of how to make a sale. It can be tiring and time consuming to work on product development and customer service because it requires a lot of communication – even on the Internet!

This is why many people avoid doing it. For now, as long as you understand that advertising is not marketing, you are on your way to better understanding how to increase your sales through organic Internet Marketing. This means that you can stop wasting time tracking all of your ads and curb the amount of money that you spend on the Internet Advertising.

About Internet Public Relations

Along with Organic Internet Marketing, Public Relations is another cost-effective way to get the word out, and every once in a while, the most effective. However, with the amount of news and opinions on the Internet, it can be hard to get noticed through a PR piece. Public Relations is simply the function of reporting on anything newsworthy that your company does. This can be almost anything, including a new website launch, a new product, a record year of sales, a contest, a new partnership, or a charity event.

When dealing with the print and broadcast media, Public Relations is generally used to heighten awareness, however, Public Relations articles on the Internet are submitted to directories and used to boost rankings. Most people only glance through them, so the most important part of Public Relations on the Internet is to help people find your web site if they are interested what you are doing.

True Story: I once worked as a credit manager for a small hotel in a major tourist destination. The Marketing Director was forever trying to get more sales from the Internet with okay success, but never really getting any substantial results. One day, this marketing director wondered out loud what the difference was between Advertising, Marketing, and Public Relations.

The marketing director of the hotel really didn't know. That when I realized that it's easy for anybody to mistake one for the other, which is why so many people spend money on advertising. Obviously, this is something you can figure out for yourself; but if someone that you work with is in charge of your advertising and marketing, it might be worth your while to ask them and see what kind of answer they give you.

Chapter Two

The right products are part of a *supply chain*.

Now that you have a basic concept of what marketing is, it's time to think about how Internet marketing will sell your product. Whether you have an existing product that you want to start selling on the Internet; an existing web site with products where you want to increase sales; or a product in your head that you think the world needs, the marketing techniques to sell on the Internet are the same as anywhere else.

If you think there is some kind of secret, there isn't. You just have to apply the same marketing principles you would apply in any other situation where you would want to increase sales. The only difference is that with the Internet, you have to learn the technology, but there are plenty of free websites to help you do that.

As far Internet Marketing is concerned, all products are also the same. So if you don't have a product, but are still yearning to sell on the

Internet, be careful. There are plenty of people out there who are willing to take all of your capital to help you 'develop' a product, including web hosting companies.

Don't Buy Other People's Products in Order to Sell Your Own

If you don't know what you want to sell, you won't be successful at marketing it anywhere. People offering advice about selling products on the Internet in exchange for $300-$500 are focused on the same thing you are – they want to make a quick buck. And they usually do – from your wallet. Also, beware of people who try to sell you their products for you to resell on the Internet. The technology may be different, but it is still a classic pyramid scheme.

Unfortunately, there is a lot of misguided free advice as well. If you read an article on someone's blog that starts talking about how to choose a product to market on the Internet, they are selling something as well. It may not be so obvious, but there is a product to buy from them in there somewhere, even if it just means having to look at all of the advertising they are selling on their site.

If someone starts talking about the steps to take about how to pick a product that's right for you, point your browser somewhere else. You can't sit down and pick a sellable product by thinking about turning your hobbies into a home-based business, or by supplying a new product that isn't available on the Internet, or by distributing a product that you think everyone will love or need.

Either you have a legitimate product to sell, and a solid business plan to go with it or you don't. The Internet is not some magic place to make money instantly - unless you are a scam artist. So unless you have a solid product that you have already worked out, even the most brilliant Internet marketing plan won't help you make sales.

There are no New Products on the Internet

Every product is already available on the Internet. The Internet is a global marketplace where capitalism still dominates because no one government can quite figure out how to regulate it. With the Internet reaching almost everyone in the world with a credit card, you can bet that there is a product for every possible need. In fact, even for the most obscure items that you can think of, there will probably be 100 different websites that are selling it. This takes some of the wind out of the sails of people who are trying to come up with new products, because even if it is only a concept in someone's mind, your product already exists somewhere out there in the world. This may seem like a lot of competition, but on the Internet, there is always room for one more e-commerce venture.

So if you don't have a product, don't try to create a market and then create a product to sell to that market because it won't work long enough to produce any significant revenue. Instead, sit down the old-fashioned way and work on a product that means something to you, even if it doesn't look like a money maker. A business plan will help you figure out if your product is worth it or not. Business plans are free on the Internet and will save you a lot of money and heartache.

So You already Have a Product

Now, let's talk about what you can do with an existing product to increase sales on the Internet, or anywhere else for that matter. Most people who have problems with sales or increasing sales have a problem with understanding their product. When you go with the premise that everything is already sold on the Internet and that there are so many successful people selling these products, the first inclination is to assume that something is wrong with your product if it isn't selling. However, this is rarely the case. It's really more a matter of understanding the product that you already have in order to create sales.

Having a cohesive product or line of products is the first thing to think about when you want to increase sales. Let's look at the super-competitive world of computer software. Whether you just sell computer software or develop it, you are going to have a product that is similar to everyone else's because software development and sales is a global effort. So what you need to think about is how your product works with other computers and software.

Remember, unless you work for a huge corporation like Microsoft or Apple, your products will have to be compatible with everyone else's. This means first finding out what kinds of computers your software will work with, and what types of computers have enough storage for your software. You will also need to make sure that your software will work in most operating systems and that you can easily take files from your software and send them to other programs and vice versa. For every software program and computer that your product doesn't work with, you will be losing customers, and there is no amount of marketing that will convince anyone to buy a product with obvious limitations.

As well, you should have a complimentary line of products to go with your software. This can include items like tutorials, books, templates, graphics, or anything else that might go with your software. If you can't come up with a unified line of complimentary products, consider partnering with someone else.

For another example, if you sell silver jewelry, and want to expand your product line without making another investment, look for someone like a watch distributer that you can partner with on the Internet. This can work to your advantage in several ways.

By providing reciprocal links to another jewelry site, you boost your rankings and also make yourself look like more of an authority on all types of jewelry. Using this kind of cohesive approach to inventory works with any types of goods or services that you might be selling. Another good example is a regional dog groomer who may partner with a breeder and a national pet supply company to boost rankings and provide more services without making any more investments in other related businesses.

Distribution is Key to Internet Sales

Distribution of your products is another major factor of Internet marketing. Whether or not you sell your product or service will depend on how your product is going to get to your buyer. In the case of computer software or games you can just download them, but what if you have a product that has to be shipped? If someone can buy your product at a local brick and mortar store, this is a huge consideration. The cost of shipping and returns can be a major stumbling block when it comes to sales.

If you can't offer free shipping and returns, you may be able to work out a deal with a shipping company, but don't count on it. In the case of shipping and returns you will have to price your items so that part of the shipping is offset by the price of the product. One way many companies do this is to make a 'buy one get another at a discount' offer, because generally the cost to ship two items at one time is cheaper.

An entirely different product distribution problem is destinations. If you are marketing a destination on the Internet like a restaurant, a hotel, or even a tourist area like a city on the Internet, make sure that people can get there to take advantage of your offers. There is nothing like offering hotel discounts, new menu items, or an event like a festival if people can't get there. Make sure that airlines, public transportation, and car rental companies are available to provide cheap fares, or you will not increase your business, no matter how good the offer is.

Suppliers are always tricky to work with, even if you make your own product. This is really marketing 101, but you still have to think about having enough product. It's one thing to have a supplier cancel out one item, but if you are a distributer for a company that stops manufacturing altogether, you may be in trouble. Any web site will have a certain ranking and amount of traffic, and if you have to shut down completely, you will have lost all of your Internet marketing efforts. This is another reason why it is important to be diversified with a cohesive and complimentary line of products. More than anything, it is important that you keep your rankings and traffic, no matter what you are selling.

The Price Has to be Right

The right price for your product is also something to consider when it comes to Internet marketing. When you own a brick and mortar store, you have much more freedom to set the price of your goods and services, especially if you are the only store in the area. However, on the Internet, your customer is a click away from finding your same product cheaper.

You may or may not be able to negotiate a price with your supplier, but chances are that someone else will buy more than you and get a better deal. So what can you do?

The first thing that you can do is specifically target one segment of the population. If you sell books for example, only sell murder mystery novels for adults. This kind of specific product lends itself incredibly well to Internet marketing because there are hundreds of web sites devoted to specific topics like murder mystery novels. If this is something you are truly interested in, becoming a regular blogger and article poster on this specific subject can help you create a substantial amount of back links to your site and boost your rankings and traffic.

You can sell rare volumes, new authors, signed additions, related movies, etc. The possibilities in a niche market are endless, and if you set yourself up as the expert, customers will come to you first. A niche Internet marketing plan also lends itself to partnering with others devoted to a particular type of product, which also reduces the competition.

The other thing that you can do if you can't meet the price of your competitors is to offer more services with your product. One marketing idea that works well on the Internet is to have an online 'expert' who can answer questions about your product with instant messages. You can have many responses already in a data base on your site which will come up when prompted, and the rest can be handled by a few people. Many people will buy from you just because they want that live interaction with a human being that other sites might not offer. This is a more economical idea if you can't afford a 1-800 number and a customer service center.

Always Take Time to Come Up With the Right Price

The pricing of your product is absolutely essential. When you consider the fact that a potential customer can have your website open on their browser at the same time as several others, comparison shopping hits a new level. This situation would make it seem like unless you have the lowest price, you won't get the sale. While this is true in some cases, many people are looking for what they consider to be the 'right' price. Figuring out the right price has a lot to do with niche marketing, so it works well for small businesses that are trying to sell to a specific audience.

When you are selling to a niche market audience, the price of your product has to be in the right price range in order for your customers to buy. For example, if you sell purely processed, high-end vitamins, they need to be priced accordingly. If you price them too low, the people you are trying to sell them to will think they are poor quality and not purchase them. So if you think that you are competing with discount vitamin warehouses, you aren't. Even if another company were to sell the same product as you, you still don't have to drop your price; you simply have to provide the perception that your product is still a better value.

Some marketing gurus call this finding a 'magic' price. While many companies will price something using the .99 cent philosophy – $4.99 looks cheaper than $5.00 – the magic price philosophy puts a perceived and imaginary value on a product. If your competitor sells a product for $13.99, you can sell the same product for $15.26. Because of the Internet, consumers are entirely price savvy, so a person looking at your website will have to wonder, why is their product $15.26? Is it better? Is it from a better source? What am I missing here?

This is the time when a better looking website, better content, and more offered services will help you get the higher or 'magic' price. This is because you are no longer competing with other vendors over who has the lowest price. You are competing over perceived value, and since you have the slightly higher price, your product has the higher value. Another reason to have a higher price is that you can always mark slow moving products down to sell to bargain hunters later and still get a better price than your competitors.

Products can also be seasonal. If you have a seasonal product, it's very difficult to try to maximize your profit during the time when it is not popular in your part of the world. Once again, the Internet works naturally with seasonal products because there is a need for products that can be purchased internationally at any time. This doesn't even mean that you have to ship worldwide; it just means that you have the opportunity to sell throughout the year on the Internet, and you should take advantage of this.

Here are some things to consider about the international sale of seasonal products:

- Know how to repackage last year's merchandise so it is attractive to buyers
- If you can't go to a sales convention for your industry, go to their website
- Strike a deal with similar merchants for their overstock
- Remember to get all of your publicity out 3 months before your season arrives
- Be aware of international holidays where your local merchandise can be used out of season

As you can see, there is a lot to plan for when it comes to developing a product that will continually sell on the Internet. There are a lot of products out there and a lot of competition. Just remember, you cannot market anything and make a long term profit that is not a solid and well-thought out idea.

This is also a good time to look into putting together a marketing plan or a business plan. These are prepared documents, usually to get business loans, where you have to answer a lot of hard-hitting questions. If you search for the words 'marketing plan' or 'business plan' on the Internet, you will get a pretty good idea of what one looks like, and also how far ahead you have to plan to stay afloat on the Internet.

Once you have a solid idea, everything else can be put into place including a business plan which will include a sellable product. Once you are sure that your product line is put together or reworked so it is sellable, you are ready to think about a sales approach.

True Story: When I first started writing Internet copy, I worked for a computer group that promised number-one rankings and heavy traffic for web sites. One client, a chemist who had developed his own brand of basement sealer, canceled his account after getting number-one through number-three rankings on the major search engines for four months in a row.

He canceled because although he had the rankings, he claimed he has no sales. Out of curiosity, I did some basic research on my own and found that there were hundreds of different formulas for basement sealers, all claiming to be unique, and most of them available locally through home improvement centers.

With no unique product, no special pricing, no complimentary products, no special services, and no niche marketing on the part of the website, there was no demand for his products, even with high rankings. This is a great example of how important it is to work on your product before you work on rankings and web traffic.

Chapter Three

Solid ecommerce starts with a *mission statement.*

When you have a genuine product, you don't have to trick anyone into buying it. Getting rankings by tricking the search engines isn't necessary if you have a solid product, a well constructed business plan, and the right Internet marketing tools. You can read hundreds of articles about the evolution of the search engines and where the 'experts' think they are going in order to fool them, but do you really want to run your business that way?

Think of the Search Engines as Being the Traffic Cops of the Internet

Everyone gets away with something every once in a while, but would you really want there to be complete chaos on the Internet? Without the search engines, there would be no organization and no logical way to find anyone. So, if you run across web developers who try to convince you to buy their services based on the premises of getting you high rankings, they can probably do it – but don't be surprised if they use some underhanded tricks to get them- and you can bet that your rankings will drop as soon as stop paying for them.

This still leaves you in the place of having low rankings and no improved sales when you hire someone to fool the search engines. It is much better to learn how to get rankings on your own and develop an Internet marketing campaign that won't fall flat on its face once you stop using artificial ways to get rankings.

A large part of this process starts with what kind of language you are going to use to sell your product. On the Internet, most of your communication will be through your website or your ecommerce store, so this will mean a lot of written communication. Written communication on the Internet is the key to Internet marketing success, because this is how the search engines evaluate whether or not you are an expert on what you are selling and whether or not to direct traffic to your site.

The search engines are essentially the traffic directors of the Internet, so if you are serious about selling a product, you don't want to invest a lot of effort into fooling them. You want the search engines to direct the most amount of real buyers to your site so that you will make the most sales.

When web developers start talking about directing traffic to your site, they will mention terms like Search Engine Optimization, keyword density, Black Hat, White Hat, etc, etc. If you have read about this and you tend to get lost, don't worry about it. Most of what they are talking about is the correct use of the English language and how it should be used to help potential buyers find your web site.

This is because the Internet is organized sort of like a giant library. Just like a library, all of the web sites are organized by name and number, so that they can be found by search engines. And just like when you go to the library, you want to locate the book with the subject matter that most relates to what you want to find. So the Internet will rank your website based on the content on the pages of your site and how they relate to the other web sites containing the same subject matter on the Internet.

What this means is that all of the words on your website have the potential to make your website more of an authority than the others, consequently bringing more buyers to your web site.

The Importance of a Mission Statement

This makes the content, mission statement, or sales pitch on your web site much more critical than you might think. Because not only are you trying to sell a product, you are also trying to get the search engines to direct more buyers to your web site at the same time. Now if your first impulse in developing your sales strategy on your web site is to be heavily invested in flash, video, clever graphics, audio, etc. you will soon realize that having a three ring circus of media on your web site won't convince anyone to buy your product or listen to your message - because they won't find your website.

This is because search engines can't categorize graphics to let buyers know where you are; they can only read words. Many people got to web developers when their overwhelming graphics don't work to get rankings and they don't understand why. That is when a web developer can take advantage and sell you bad content, bad links, and other tricks that will work temporarily, but not in the long run.

It is better to develop a sales strategy in the early stages of any Internet marketing campaign because once you decide how you want to sell your product, the keywords that you need to attract the search engines attention will be easier to figure out. So logically, once you have a product in mind, you need to develop a sales pitch or mission statement before you start developing your website and deciding how you are going to promote it on the Internet. That makes it easier to pick out keywords that you can use to get the rankings and traffic that you need to make sales.

People publish web sites and open e-stores for many different reasons, but in order to sell to people you have to decide what yours is. Whatever the reason, you need to be clear about exactly what it is you want to accomplish and what is different about your site that offers something that people can't get anywhere else. You may be selling the same product as everyone else, but there has to be a reason why you are doing this.

For example, if you want to sell a product like t-shirts, there are thousands of websites that also sell them. You have to decide all of the reasons why you have decided to sell whatever kind of t-shirts you are selling and write a mission statement and a sales pitch before you start developing a web site and an Internet marketing campaign.

This mission statement and sales pitch will become the foundation for your company and give you a distinctive presence on the web. There is stiff competition for every product that is out there, and you have to decide what makes your product so special that customers will choose to buy from your online store over everyone else's.

Here are some questions to answer that will help get you started:

- Who is my target audience or demographic?
- Why would someone buy this product from my company instead of going somewhere else?
- What benefits does my customer get from me that they can't get anywhere else?
- What extra services can I provide that will make this purchase special?
- What kind of people am I trying to reach?
- What kind of people can I expect to respond to my company and its products?
- How much are people willing to pay for my product?
- How far am I willing to go to make these people happy and loyal to my products?
- What kind of quality do I want to portray as a company?

After you write down the answers to these questions, you will not only have a better idea of who you are trying to reach; you will also have the type of language that you may want to include on the homepage of your website.

The home page of your web site is the first page that people will glance at to get an idea of whether you have what they are look for on the Internet. So your answers should be clear and concise, because you only have about ten seconds to let viewers know what your website is about.

That is why you have to be careful with using too many graphics and other distractions like flash and audio. This is because while someone may be entertained by your presentation - if they can find your message - they'll keep right on surfing.

You can go a step further to narrow down who you want to buy your products. This marketing theory is old as well, but it still applies when you want to figure out who is going to buy from you.

The Theory is That There are Four Types of Buyers:

- Those who want to be the first to buy something
- Those who are cautious and want to see someone else buy first
- Those who have to be convinced to buy
- Those who will always be the last to buy something.

For example, if you sell sunglasses, there will always be the person who has to have the new style before everyone else. Maybe it's some sort of addiction, buy they will always be the first one on the block to have something new for bragging rights.

Then you will have the followers, who simply purchase new sunglasses to keep up with the trendsetters. They convince their other friends to buy, so then finally, you have the person who won't buy anything unless they absolutely feel they have to do so. These are also the customers who want a discount. Think about these types of customers and how it applies to your business.

If you are still stumped by what to say about yourself or your company, always check out the competition. However, never copy anyone, because search engines won't acknowledge duplicate content on the Internet. So when you copy somebody, you aren't doing yourself any favors. Always remember, you are trying to appeal to the search engines as much as you are trying to appeal to customers and clients.

You can check out the competition simply by typing related key words into the dialogue box on your browser. If you want to sell t-shirts, for example, search for words like 'cotton t-shirts', 'children's t-shirts', 'logo t-shirts' or any words that have to do with the t-shirts that you may be selling.

If you notice, there are going to be a list of the top ranked sites that come up in the search results, but then there are probably about 40 more pages of results after that. The Internet has some pretty stiff competition. In addition to getting some ideas about what to say in your sales pitch or mission statement, now is also a good time to go through your competitor's web sites and look at what they are selling.

Then Ask Yourself Some Questions Like:

- What kind of products do they have?
- What are their price points?
- What is their return policy?
- How much is shipping?
- What kind of payments do they take?
- Do they have a toll-free phone number?
- How is their site set up?
- Etc, etc, etc.

Don't let it intimidate you that there is so much competition. By going through your competitor's web sites, you will notice that there are a lot of websites that don't put a lot of effort into their marketing. They rely on graphics and flash to sell their product, but many consumers are way too savvy to fall for that kind of a sales pitch anymore; and the only reason you may come across half of these websites is because you are specifically looking for them. Keep focused on looking at what kind of language other businesses are using to sell a similar product, and think about how that would work in your situation.

True Story: I recently got a project that involved editing one of those 'secrets of how to get rich quick on the Internet' books. While this was paid editing work for me, I was really curious as to what this person had to say.

Who knows, maybe I would quit writing for the Internet and make some easy money. Anyway, the book, along with the cd's cost almost $600.00. So, I was definitely intrigued and thought I might get a free education while I got paid to edit a book.

It turns out that the book was about how to take the marketing ideas from other people on the Internet and repackage the ideas to sell them to other people who wanted to get rich quick as well.

Talk about a pyramid scheme. Suffice it to say, no matter how tempted you are, skip the expensive books, seminars, and cd's that are about how to get rich quick on the Internet. This is because I can tell you first-hand that all of this kind of useless information is always a scam.

Chapter Four

When you have a product, you can brand *your website*.

Branding a product, service, company, or idea for the purpose of marketing it on the Internet centers on developing a website; and developing a successful website wholly relies on picking the right domain name. However, it's important to understand the concept of branding first, which will help you create a marketable domain name.

If you already have a brick and mortar store, a company, or a product - choosing a domain name is fairly easy. That is, if it isn't already taken as a domain name by someone else. However, if your made-up brand name doesn't reflect what you do as a company or as a person, and also isn't selling, you might want to start over again, or at least develop a new and totally separate sales approach.

The Internet is absolutely forgiving in the fact that you can start up an entirely new marketing plan with almost no money. Even if your first attempts are a failure, you can do some really productive market research with less than a couple hundred dollars.

The formula for branding on the Internet is an easy one to remember: Branding = Sales = Marketing = Domain Name

It's all the same thing, and while all of the elements are equal in their importance, they are also equally inseparable. You'll notice that you don't see advertising in this formula. This is because advertising doesn't equal sales. This is why ecommerce owners get so frustrated when they are throwing advertising dollars at a bad brand name or bad marketing idea. It's because advertising a bad brand doesn't do anything to help sales. Always remember, advertising can solidify your brand name (domain name) but it has nothing to do with sales.

Why Branding is Important

Branding is important because these days, most products are bought, not sold. Let's face it; you don't have much opportunity to directly sell to Internet viewers. It's not like you can convince anyone to buy something with a sales letter; although many sales people still try.

Consumers delete emails faster than they throw out hard-copy junk mail, and yet there are so many entrepreneurs looking for the exactly right language to convince someone to buy. No one falls for sales pitches anymore; they fall for brands, and you have to make your brand name more appealing than anyone else's brand name on the Internet. So your main goal when it comes to Internet marketing should be to make your name stand out from all others in your market.

In other words, branding means singularity, and your brand is your unique identity and also essentially your name. Traditionally, brand names are proper nouns that are capitalized, but on the Internet, lowercase, mixed case, and any kind of font works as long as it is recognized globally.

A domain name should be easy to remember, easy to spell, and easy to read. Especially if you want global business, your brand name should be recognized in any language. So, for example, if you sell hard-to-find auto parts over the Internet, it may not help to have the word auto in your name if people who do not speak English want to buy your product. As well, with auto in your domain name, you don't separate yourself from anyone else on the Internet, which defeats the purpose of branding.

Having a generic noun like 'auto' in your domain name or brand name means that you will have a whole lot more advertising to do to try to get potential buyers to pay attention. This entirely defeats the purpose of having people buy from you because you are different.

A much better marketing strategy for someone selling hard-to-find auto parts would be to name the company and the domain name after themselves. It is relatively easy to personalize a site when you profile one individual who is an expert at finding even the most obscure auto parts through an entire network of auto auctions, car lots, and salvage yards around the globe.

This kind of brand name also lends itself to article submission, an important part of search engine optimization. With a person who is a salvage expert at the helm of a website, you can easily write fresh content for article submissions on a regular basis. So instead of the domain name 'Used Part Auto King', it will appeal more to a niche market to use the domain name 'Shaunessy's'.

In the context of this book, it might not sound so appealing, but if this name were really used in association with used auto parts; it would eventually be the first place someone would look on the Internet for this product. Think about all of the stores that you love that are named after a fictitious person. Why do you go there? Because you have been conditioned to associate that name with exactly what you are looking for. That's branding.

Getting the Right Domain Name

A good domain name becomes the driving force behind any successful web site. A good domain name can not only drive traffic to your website, it can also become the name that everyone remembers when they think of a certain product or idea. A good domain name becomes a recognized brand name which automatically sells itself to consumers.

Also, there are thousands of websites out there that you will be competing with for sales. You don't want to be constantly competing for rankings as well because it takes too much time. If you have a generic word like 'auto' as the main focus of your domain name or brand name, you will be directly competing with all of the other thousands of people who thought that putting the word 'auto' in their domain name would work for them too.

As cheap as it is to start a web site, you'll be constantly taking time to get better rankings, which is a fight that you can't win with generic keywords. It is much better to stick with an individual and easy to remember name. Besides, to get higher rankings through Search Engine Optimization, you will be using the word 'auto' in your content most of the time, which will support your brand name anyway and make people think of you when they see the word auto.

A specific brand name, unlike a generic brand name also keeps your company focused. If you associate your domain name with your personal name or a fictional name that you are branding, people will think of your product when they think of your name. This will also keep your product line specific. You want a specific product line because you will sell more on the Internet that way.

Going back to the auto parts example, it might make sense for the owner to expand to selling reconditioned appliance parts as well in order to make more money on one web site. This kind of move actually hurts sales because the people who trust this brand name for auto parts lose faith as the association with auto parts weakens and become mixed in with appliance parts.

If more sales are wanted from one brand name or web site having to do with auto parts, it would be better to expand the line by selling something like manuals on how to install vintage auto parts written by the owner. This is because these two products complement each other. If you are buying vintage auto parts, chances are that you need the installation manual that goes with it. The customer gets everything what they want in one stop and the company makes more sales without weakening the brand name.

Strengthening Your Brand Name

Focusing on your domain name and associating it with one product will strengthen your brand name because you will become an expert on your subject matter and become the place to go for anything concerning your product. So if you sell hard-to–find auto parts, instruction manuals on how to install them, reconditioned auto parts, original stereos for older cars, original hardware, customized auto parts, discontinued hood ornaments, etc. - you become the recognized authority for people who restore cars. This branding strategy works for any product that you are selling.

A brand name or domain name should also be a symbol of the kind of quality that you are selling. If you want to sell your product for a higher price, you have to have a high quality name. Especially if you are selling something like jewelry, the name says everything. You can try to sell a product like jewelry on the Internet cheaper than anyone else, but unless you have a pretty fantastic supplier, this may not be a good idea.

Instead, it is much better to come up with a brand name that reflects the personality of the jewelry you are selling. It really shouldn't have the word jewelry in it, because you are already cheapening the name of your brand and blending in with all of the other jewelry companies on the Internet. It's better to have a name that makes your jewelry sound special.

This will make it easier to write content for your website and also subsequent articles. It will also make it easier to pick out keywords for search engine optimization purposes. Your domain name or brand name should be consistent with your pricing, your product, and all of the communication that you use in your marketing. Customers will buy form you based on the idea that you have higher quality merchandise than other vendors, even if you don't.

One of the most worrisome aspects of branding is designing a logo and the typography or font that goes with it. Thinking about this will probably give you no end of grief, but with a solid marketing plan, your logo, typography, and the colors that you choose to brand your company aren't as important as you think. As far as most advertising executives will tell you, there are a few steadfast rules that apply; but other than that, the Internet hasn't been around long enough for anyone to evaluate the effect of logos on sales.

Here Are Some Basic Advertising Rules for Your Logo:

- The typography (font) on your logo must be easy to read.
- Horizontal logos are more effective than vertical ones.
- The colors of your logo and your web site will set a mood.

Other than that, there are no hard and fast rules that apply. You can find people with advice like 'the color red makes people hungry' and 'the color blue calms them down', and that factors like these must somehow influence people to purchase your product. You can get worked up about this all that you want, but the fact of the matter is, if you make this the main focus of your Internet marketing campaign, you are really missing the boat.

People are going to buy your product based on the confidence they have in you and your company. They are not going to be mesmerized or rolled over by a logo. If they were, they wouldn't be surfing the Internet at 10 web sites per minute.

Think about it this way. Let's say you have a travel site that sells Caribbean vacations – the first graphics that a viewer will look for is blue water, a yellow sun, and palm trees to make sure they have the right kind of web site. They glance at your logo, they look for a destination, they look for a price, and then they move on if the price isn't right. That's it.

So instead of over-agonizing yourself over a logo and the color theme of your site, it would be better just to go with your gut and spend more time on the most important part of your website – the product and the price.

Branding your domain name also means giving it credentials.

Credibility is the acceptance that consumers must have in order to buy your product, and that credibility comes from credentials. In the case of a brick and mortar store that starts selling on the Internet, their credentials come from the fact that people shop there and know them to have a reliable product first hand. If you only have an ecommerce store, however, where do your credentials come from? In other words, why would someone trust you?

It's easy. Your credentials will come from a slogan that you place on your website. It's weird logic but it's true. Think about it. If you see the brand name or logo of a successful grocery store, along with it, you will see a slogan like, "Americas' Favorite Grocery Store", or "The Best Produce on Earth."

This grocery store may have a good product, but it's highly doubtful that everyone in America took a vote and decided that this grocery store was everyone's favorite, and even less likely that there is a way to determine what constitutes the planet Earth's best produce. And yet, there it is - an unsubstantiated and improbable statement right next to their name.

No one can disprove what they are saying, so every consumer just accepts it. In fact, they may shop at that particular grocery store specifically because it has the best vegetables on Earth. Because no one cares to dispute the statement, it becomes true and credible. Always having a slogan that goes with your brand name is best way to give yourself instant credibility and instant sales.

One last thing about branding on the Internet is the perception of where customers and clients can contact you. You may be reaching a global audience, but you are doing so from a particular location. If you are selling designer clothing, for example, having a New York address and phone number makes you extremely credible. But what if you have an address in Wisconsin?

This is a place that is extremely well-known for dairy products, but what if you are selling cocktail dresses? Even just saying it here in this book doesn't sound so plausible. The point here is that if you sell something that doesn't go with the area that you live, it is worth mentioning why you are located where you are and why this is advantageous to the consumer.

For example, "There are many clothing manufacturers in Madison, so I can get you the best deals on designer clothing." This will make sense to most consumers and make them more likely to buy from you.

True Story: When I was writing copy for an SEO company, we got
the contract for a company who sold diet pills. Keeping in mind that they sold the same diet pills that you can get at any drugstore, department store and anywhere on the Internet, I tried to write the copy so it had some personality that would make it stand out.

I wrote keyword-optimized copy, and the diet pill vendor got the rankings, but there was no increase in sales. The company had a generic name with the word diet in it, no cheaper pricing than anyone else, and no kind of slogan to give it credibility. My first thought was that we could rewrite the copy to make them stand out more as a company, but that wasn't what they wanted. To them, the problem was the graphics that the web designer was using on their site.

After six weeks of trying to find just the right color, blue background and perfect fitness model, and with no improvement in sales, the diet pill distributor cancelled their contract with the SEO Company. The diet company could never understand that it was the message and credibility, along with the rankings that would sell their diet products —not colors and graphics. Once again, this is a real company that lost all of their sales because they put the emphasis on advertising instead of marketing and branding.

Chapter Five

Web hosting companies can help market *your product.*

Cheap web hosting companies have provided an incredible marketing opportunity for anyone who wants to start a small business and has little or no money for marketing. Imagine it. Starting for as low as $5 a month, you can have your own website!

It's an incredible opportunity as long as you are willing to learn and do most of the work yourself. But if you believe in your product and you like the idea of being your own boss, having your own website is something that is too good to pass up. Even if you work for a company and have the opportunity to get involved with the website part of the business because of cutbacks, dive in and take the opportunity to learn for your own benefit to master Internet Marketing.

Assuming that you are going to have a website as part of your Internet Marketing plan, it is time to start designing it. If you don't know anything about web site development, don't panic. It isn't as hard to learn as you might think. Like everything else that has to do with computers, it's been upgraded to point-and-click technology.

There are a lot of web developers who will tell you that you need their services and a lot of computer coding to get any rankings, but this simply isn't true. Ask any web developer if they have a computer science degree. If they don't, you'll understand that web development is something that anyone can learn if they make a little effort. If you get stuck with technical glitches or have questions, any technical information you need is free on the Internet.

The Two Steps to Creating a Website

There are two steps to developing your site; building it and then publishing it. Building your site refers to creating web pages and filling them with text and graphics. Publishing your site means actually putting it out on the Internet where web browsers can find it and open the pages for viewers to look at.

If you have no idea whatsoever about web design and are completely overwhelmed, there are an incredible amount of point-and-click website builders available.

A site builder is a computer program that contains everything you need to set up and publish a website. Almost every web hosting company provides a site builder for free, and despite what you have heard, they are fine for someone who is just learning. Besides, why would you pay a lot of money for someone to design a web site for a product that you aren't even sure is going to sell?

The free sites builders are limited with regards to coding and other features like drop-down menus, but if you want a website that does more, there is a lot of software that you can buy to develop web sites that use point-and-click methods. This kind of software can be expensive, but it will definitely help you design a more powerful website on your own.

Creating a Navigable Website

The most important thing when it comes to Internet marketing with regards to website design is that your sight must be navigable. A navigable web site means that someone can get around your site easily and find everything they need to make a purchase. So even though it's tempting, by overloading your website with lots of graphics and flash, you may be making it harder for someone to make a purchase from you.

Simpler is always better, since the main thing that people want to see is if you have their product and if you have it for the right price. Your graphics may not have even down loaded before someone has moved on to another site because they don't' immediately see what they want from you.

Also, be aware that if you expect to sell to people in a rural area that they may have slow Internet service and you may be putting yourself at a distinct disadvantage with too many graphics to download.

With any site builder, you will notice that there are templates to get you started and they are divided into categories like office templates, retail templates, services templates, etc. They are organized this way because each website needs to be structured according to the way that each different business operates and what it is offering.

To this effect, a jewelry store will be set up with products, prices, and descriptions, while a doctor's office will have a list of services, resources and doctors. Remember, a potential customer will leave your site in a few seconds if they can't find what they are looking for, so being able to navigate your site easily is absolutely paramount to making a sale.

Any one of these templates may not be all encompassing for your particular business, but they are a great start to understanding how a website should be laid out and how it should be linked together. You can also look at other websites in your industry to get even more ideas. You will see a definite organization for each different kind of business. For example, a doctor's office will have a welcome page, an 'about us' page, a doctor's credentials page, a directions page, and a form page where you can request more information or book an appointment.

This may sound over-simplified, but you will notice that on the template, there is a tab on the home page for every other web page and only one purpose for each page. This makes it easy for a person to figure out where they need to go to find what they need at a glance.

Since web sites are organized by pages, designing your site on paper is a good way to see what your web site will look like before you start working with a template.

Most web developers use a simple spiral notebook to organize their thoughts and draw out the website beforehand. That's right, a spiral notebook. So you see, web development isn't as sophisticated as it would seem.

Just take as many sheets of paper as you need and make each sheet of paper a page on your web site. Set up each page as a mock-up of what it will look like when it will be published on the Internet. Include elements like your logo, any artwork, products shots, product descriptions, any text or other content, links, a shopping cart, drop down menus, active buttons, or any other technical elements that will be part of your site.

You can even go so far as to lay your pages out on a table or put them up on the wall; then you can get an impression of what your site will look like and how a visitor might get around it.

The Welcome Page is Going to Become the Most important Page

Not only is the homepage the place on your web site that grants access to all of the other pages, here is where your mission statement, along with the first impression of your product and its price will be. No matter what video, audio or flash a welcome page has on it, people will leave immediately if the mission statement doesn't contain the information they are looking for; or even if it is too wordy.

This is because when most people read text on a web site, they scan and pick out important points. If the information they want isn't there, they leave. Working on what you say on your welcome page is much more important than having eye-popping graphics or lots of flash.

When you write the text for your welcome page, the best way to write it is in the shortest sentences possible and by using bullet points to help someone scan the page. Bullet points are lists that are scored with A, B, C's, or 1, 2, 3's, or dots.

Always put your message ahead of your graphics, because this is what marketing is, and a solid message is what will sell your product. With clear, organized wording on your welcome page, even if viewers don't make a purchase, no one will leave your web site wondering what it was about. Who knows? They may become a future sale or refer you to someone else if they know what the purpose of your website is.

True story: A local tour operator that I knew who owned a white-water rafting company had a web developer who created visually stunning, but hard to navigate website.

The site had about thirty pages and included separate pages for every price of rafting trip, further subdivided by time of year, age range pricing, group pricing, and desperate pricing for all of the extras. It also included almost every photograph possible of the surrounding state and attractions. Even the reservation people couldn't figure it out.

The price per rafting trip averaged about $75.00, so the site was way too complicated for that kind of product. There were a lot of inquiries from potential customers, but no bookings because everything had to be explained on the reservations line, making more work instead of less.

When the owner tried to take their web site back, it took them a whole season to get out of the contract and a small bundle of money to get back all of the elements of their website. They still knew nothing about web hosting and had to hire someone else.

It's not so much that the web developer did anything wrong, it's just that the tour operator outsourced the job and let someone take over this very important part of their marketing. It's okay to outsource marketing you don't have time for, but make sure that you understand what someone is doing at all time when it comes to creating or managing your web site.

Chapter Six

Choosing a web host *takes time.*

Choosing a web host for your web site requires some thought, because there are an incredible amount of affordable web hosting companies out there. Price is important, but there are a few technical aspects to look at first before you sign a contract with a hosting company.

The first thing you need to pick is a hosting platform. Picking a hosting platform or operating system may take some research on your part if you don't know anything about the technical side of web hosting. An operating system or hosting platform is the main interface between the computer hardware that your web hosting company owns and the software that you are going to use to build and manage your site.

The two operating systems platforms that you will be offered from a low cost web hosting company is most commonly Linux, with Windows at a more expensive rate. The third option may be UNIX, but it isn't really something to think about if you aren't familiar with computer code.

Windows is more expensive than Linux, but also the most easy to use and the easiest to get started with if you want to create the most professional looking web site with the least amount of computer or technical knowledge. This is because with Windows, you can us FrontPage and ASP.Net to create your site.

These are software programs developed by Windows to build a professional web site without knowing a lot about HTML code. HTML code is the code that goes on your web pages to create dynamic web pages.

The distinction between a dynamic page and a static page makes a real difference in the functionality of your web site. A static web page is merely a page that has text and images. A dynamic web pad is coded with HTML so that you can create items like interactive forms and dropdown menus.

If you are on a budget, Windows hosting can be cost-prohibitive. This is because all Windows products have licensing fees and you have to pay them. So you have to pay the fee for the operating system and for each separate program that you use in order to get the benefit of instant coding. Beware of cheaper Linux hosting companies that promise you extensions for Microsoft products that will allow them to run on a Linux operating system because it doesn't always work.

With a Linux operating system, which is more popular and much cheaper, you will either have to use the free site builder provided by the web hosting company you sign up with, or learn enough about web applications, scripting languages and data bases to be able to copy the professional capabilities of software like FrontPage.

However, if you are just starting out, either option may be a bit overwhelming, so the best thing to do may be to take the free site builder offered by you hosting company to create your first site. Think of the free site builder as a learning experience. It may not have everything that other more professional sites will have, but it will give you the chance to learn the basics of Internet marketing and make mistakes without investing a lot of money.

The next thing to think about when you choose a web hosting company is what kind of hosting package you will need. Hosting packages are usually offered on shared, virtual private server, or dedicated servers. Virtual private server and dedicated server hosting are for larger websites with more traffic and large product catalogues. With unlimited disk space and storage space, a shared hosting plan will probably be suitable for most small business websites.

What is Shared Hosting?

Here is how a shared hosting works. When you sign up for your hosting package, you will upload all of your files onto your hosting company's computer which is called the server. All of your web site information and files will be stored on the server, with the many other files of the other people who have also purchased a hosting plan from the hosting company. In short, sharing a server with other web sites is called shared hosting. This is generally the cheapest web hosting that you can find on the Internet and is perfectly fine if you are just starting out.

A shared hosting plan will also offer you a certain amount of disk storage space and bandwidth per month. Disk storage space is the amount of space you have on the server; in other words, how many web pages you can have. Data Transfer, or bandwidth, refers to how many times your site can be downloaded by viewers per month. All hosting companies limit how big your web site can be and how many users per month can visit it.

If a web hosting company offers you 1,500 GB per month of storage space and 15,000 GB per month of bandwidth, this should be more than enough to run your website. You can approximate the amount of disk space and bandwidth you need per month by adding up the amount of megabytes in your web site files. A Megabyte is approximately 1,024,000 characters, and a Gigabyte is ten times that amount, or 10,240,000. If you add up how many megabytes your files have and apply it to how much disk space your web hosting company is giving you, you can figure out how many files, documents, or data you can have on your web site. Check with your web hosting company to see if you can upgrade your hosting package if your web site needs the disk space and security of a virtual or dedicated hosting.

Other Things to Think About When Choosing a Host

You are getting closer to choosing a web host, but there are a few more things to consider. There are many reasons why you might pick one hosting company over another, but here are few more questions to ask before you sign a contract:

- Where is the data center located? (The data center houses all of the computers.)
- Where is the customer service center located? Is it outsourced?
- What kind of tech support is available if I have problems with software?
- When was the operating system software last updated or overhauled?
- How old are the servers (computers) in the data center?
- What is the guaranteed uptime policy?

The price per month, disk space, bandwidth, included features, included software, and free features will also play a part in your decision. Once you have read the contract thoroughly and asked all of the questions you need to, you are ready to sign up with a hosting company.

Submitting Your Domain Name

Submitting your domain name is an important part of signing up with an affordable web hosting company. Domain names are like phone numbers in the fact that only one person can have a domain name because it identifies who you are on the Internet.

Your web hosting company will perform a domain name search for you to make sure that no one else has your domain name and then register that domain name for you for a period of one year. You must pay for and renew your name each and every year or you will lose it. If someone has your domain name, the hosting company will make some alternative suggestions, but you will have to keep trying until you find one that is unique.

After that, you can sign the contract and pay for your website. Once you have signed the contract, you can build your web site. You will do this by using software like FrontPage, another software program, or the free site builder included in your web hosting package.

Any way you go, you don't have to panic; there will be step-by - step instructions and plenty of wizards to guide you. This is the time when you can add your pictures and other content that you have created to your web site. You can do this offline or online, and when you are finished, most hosting companies have an automatic publishing feature.

True Story: I had an assignment to write for a web hosting
package reseller who wanted me to write a consumer report on the best web hosting companies out there.

I found a lot of really bad stories out there and a lot of angry people who claimed that they had been ripped off by these web hosting companies. It seemed like there were no honest web hosting companies at all.

I kept reading customer feedback and came to the conclusion that a lot of these people had read all of the sales literature, but not the contract they had signed. These are some of the things that they were angry about:

- Unlimited disk space and bandwidth that was promised actually had a cap placed on it.
- Extensions for Windows programs on Linux operating systems didn't work as promised.
- The free domain name wasn't actually free and really belonged to the web hosting company.
- The uptime was never 99.9% or even 90%
- Unlimited emails were capped during each 24 hour period.
- The yearlong contract could not be canceled after thirty days, no matter what the circumstances.

I checked out these complaints that originated from the anti-web hosting chat rooms and compared them to the sales jargon and the contracts. I could see where these customers were angry, but at the same time, the contract had all of the language that clearly stated what the real terms of sale were.

The advice here is that when you find the web hosting company you want to sign up with, you should print out a hard copy of the contract and then you should ask the customer service people every question you have. It will give you a chance to try out the customer service department and fully understand what you are buying. This is important, because in all cases, the web hosting company went exactly by the contract and not by the sales promises.

Chapter Seven

Learning coding basics is *important*.

If you publish a website on the Internet and you want people to find it, you have to give them as many directions to get there as possible.

Focusing on pay per click advertising may seem like the best way to get people to your website, but it is really a hit or miss proposition. Putting out something like a banner ad is like putting up a billboard on the highway for a brick and mortar business. Some people will stop at your business because you got them at the right time and some people will stop because they had to; but very few people will get off the highway and patronize your establishment out of the curiosity created by your billboard.

Even a billboard that says 'Last stop for fifty miles' will only goad a certain amount of people into stopping.

The Importance of Developing a Marketing Friendly Website

Instead of pay per click advertising, it is much better to develop your web site so that you can take advantage of Internet marketing strategies like search engine optimization. This will require coding skills, so this is usually the point when companies start hiring web developers without fully understanding what they are doing.

Coding web pages to make them dynamic and so that they will function as part of your Internet marketing plan may seem daunting at first, but it is extremely import to learn, or you will always be at the mercy of web developers in order to get any significant traffic to your site.

Learning basic HTML code only takes a few hours to understand and few weeks to start using. All HTML code really involves is separating the text into sections for the browsers to read by using angle brackets (<,>).

That's it. After you learn HTML code, you will free to develop your own web pages to maximize them for use in an Internet marketing campaign. HTML stands for Hypertext Markup Language and is the markup language used to indicate the different parts of a dynamic web page. Along with Meta data, it is the code embedded in your web page that lets the search engines find and rank your web page on the Internet.

Dissecting the Parts of a Web Page

Obviously, a web site is made up of pages with text, graphics, and in many cases, interactive forms like drop down menus and rollover buttons. This is all understandable, but where many people who develop web sites for the first time get lost is being able to understand what coding their web pages means.

Putting aside all of the flash, video and other gimmicks that are put onto a website, a web page that uses HTML is divided into three parts:

- The first part is simply a line of code at the top of the page that lets the browser know what version of HTML you are using so that it can display the page to the viewer correctly.

- The second part is the header section, which tells the search engine what the page is about so that it can be ranked in a search.

- The third part of the page is the body, or the bulk of information that is included in the web page.

Why Everyone Avoids Coding Their Own Web Site

The reason why coding is such a mystery to so many people is that as computer users, we have become so used to 'What You See is What You Get' pages. When we use word processing programs, we don't understand the science behind what we are creating. So when we create a document in a 'WYSIWYG' word processing program, the science behind it is lost on us.

For example, if you want something to be written in a **bold** font, you just highlight the text and mark it **bold**. This process doesn't work so well on the Internet, because depending on what browsers are looking at your site, your text could wind up looking awful. HTML is just a way of making whatever text and graphics you are using look the same in any browser.

Here's a good analogy: If you have ever tried to open a text document created with a program on your computer in a different program on someone else's computer, you may get garbled-looking gibberish. A document opened in another program or even another version of the same program simply won't look the same way.

The First Section of the Web Page

The first section, or the HTML code at the beginning of every web page, fixes formatting problems by alerting the browser as to what version of code you are using and lets the browser make adjustments so that the page looks exactly the same as you intended.

The Second Section of the Web Page

However, HTML code does so much more than just letting your pages open the same for every browser. The second section, or the HEAD ELEMENT, is where you can put the title of your page so that the search engines can rank it. If you don't do this, every one of your web pages will have the title as your URL, or your domain name. This means that your site will only get ranked for one title on your website, which doesn't do you any good. So it is important to put a descriptive title on every page using HTML. If you have twenty pages on your web site, that means you have twenty different titles that you can rank for and twenty different titles that you can use to get back links from other sites. This will improve your rankings greatly.

Additional information is also located in the head section and is called Meta data or is sometimes referred to as Meta tags. This is information inserted into your web pages that viewers cannot see and is for the purpose of communicating with the browser.

Information in Meta tags can also communicate information to search engines so they know how to rank a page. This is why it is important to put keywords into the title of each page. Keywords put into the title of the page will further solidify the ranking of the page for the search engines.

For example, if you sell water filters, a keyword-rich title might be, "How a Whole House Water Filter Saves You Money." The search engines pick up on the words 'whole house water filter' 'saves' and 'money'; the benefit being that if someone typed these words into a search, your site would come up in the rankings.

In order to solidify the content of your article for the search engines, you will also put a description and keywords in the header area for the search engine to see.

The Third Section of the Web Page

The third, section of the web page is the body. This is where most of the text for the page goes. Putting all three elements together – the HTML tag, the head element, and the body, will create a web page that is easily browsed by the search engines. Let's look at a very simple and small article that you might write and post on your web site if you sold water filters.

This is what the page would look like on your web site:

Whole House Water Filters

Whole house water filters are healthy for any residence. There are many reasons to buy a water filter for anywhere you live. If you are in an urban area, chances are you live in an old building where the pipes may be rusty and carrying whatever is coming off of them into your drinking water filters.

If you like water straight from the tap, but own an older condominium, you might think about buying home water filters for all of your faucets. If you were to pay a plumber to replace the pipes, it could cost thousands of dollars.

Drinking water filters can remove the residue, silt, metals and other items that you may be ingesting and will save you money over hiring a plumber to replace the pipes.

Now, let's look at what kind of code it takes to produce this page. →

This same article, with all of the html code, would look like this:

<!DOCTYPE HTML PUBLIC "-//W3C//DTD HTML 4.01
Transitional//EN"
"http://www.w3.org/TR/html4/loose.dtd">   ← A
<html>   ← B
<head>   ← C
<title> Whole House Water Filters</title> ← D   ↓ E
<meta name="description" content="How A Whole House Water
Filter Saves You Money.">
<meta name="keywords" content="whole house water filters, water
filter, drinking water filters, home water filters ">   ← F
</head>
<body> ← G
Whole house water filters are healthy for any residence. There are
many reasons to buy a **water filter** for anywhere you live. If you are
in an urban area, chances are you live in an old building where the
pipes may be rusty and carrying whatever is coming off of them into
your **drinking water filters**. If you like water straight from the tap
but own an older condominium, you might think about buying **home
water filters** for all of your faucets. If you were to pay a plumber to
replace the pipes, it could cost thousands of dollars. **Drinking water
filters** can remove the residue, silt, metals and other items that you
may be ingesting and will save you money over hiring a plumber to
replace the pipes.
</body>   ← H
</html>

Here is a Key That Corresponds With the Coding Diagram:

A →The first two line of code tell the browser what version of html you are using. In this case, it is HTML 4.01

B →This code starts the page.

C →This code denotes the head section

D →This is the title of the article.

E →This is the Meta title, which tell the search engine what the article is about.

F →This Meta tag tells the search engine what the keyword for the article are.

G →This code indicates the start of the article. As you can see, every keyword that is in the Meta tag is also in the article. The keywords are highlighted for reference.

H →This code ends the body and the page.

There's a little more to it than that, but now you can get the idea. So stop being mystified by web developers and start doing the coding yourself. It will take time to figure out, but it is worth is if you want to launch a truly successful marketing campaign without spending a lot of money on web development.

If you ever want to see how a real website page is coded, just right-click on the web page and select 'View Source' on the menu that pops up. You can get a much better idea of how real coding is done.

Remember, if you have plain text word processing software, you can write HTML code. This will be something like 'Notepad' which comes with every computer and is located in accessories. You can't use any software that uses point and click 'What You See Is What You Get' technology because it will put code into your document that you don't want.

This leaves out most other word processing programs, even though they will try to sell you on their web capabilities. There are hundreds of free tutorials on the Internet that will take you step-by-step to learn HTML. There is also free HTML software available.

A lot of people will try to get you buy software that build websites for you and puts in all of your coding. The programs are okay, but a lot of the coding can be wrong; and even though the page looks all right - if the coding is wrong, your rankings will suffer. It is better to do the coding yourself and make sure that is search-engine-friendly. However, you should always validate your coding. You do this by checking with W3C, the organization charged with designing and maintaining the HTML language. This service is free, and will make sure that your coding is search-engine-friendly.

As well, PHP can be embedded into dynamic web pages. PHP is a term that you will come across in many different contexts when it comes to web hosting. PHP (or Hypertext Preprocessor) is one of the many open-source (free) scripting language that was invented to create dynamic web pages that is developed and updated by the free software community, PHP Group.

PHP works well on a Linux hosting platform and will save you from buying a lot of expensive web development software if you want dynamic web pages. Your web host's server will also recognize PHP code that is embedded in web pages by the angle brackets (<,>).

While PHP is a little more difficult to learn than HTML, it opens up a lot of other possibilities when it comes to creating and processing dynamic web pages, and is much better to use in the long run than software that writes the code for you.

When you sign up with your web hosting company, you should also look for other computer languages, scripts, and software like MySQL, FTP, Apache, Python, Perl, Java, Joomla, Cron, Fantastico, ASP, CGI, and Ruby on Rails that should be included in your hosting package.

You won't know what all of these mean right off the bat, but you will eventually them need if you go on to build your own website. It is better to get scripting languages that come with a hosting package because they will be configured to work specifically with that web company's operating system.

Remember, the operating system is the interface that lets the software work with the computer. Many of the problems that people who are new to web hosting have is when they try to introduce third party software to a web hosting company's operating system.

True Story: When I started writing content pages and articles freelance for the Internet, I had no idea what coding was. Generally, I would write the content and the buyer would code it to put on their website.

Web development was hard for me to understand because many web writers assume you are already familiar with it. They tend to jump right in and start throwing around terminology that is almost impossible to understand.

Times have changed, and not only do web masters want articles, but they wanted them coded as well. It took a really understanding client and about a week for me to learn about coding; but I did it, and now it's easy. I realized that the biggest fear I had was not being smart enough to understand computer programming, but is turns out that being afraid was the biggest obstacle to learning about coding a website.

So here is some more information about dynamic web pages to make things a little bit clearer:

Dynamic web pages were first introduced in the mid 90's when a Danish web developer started working with a set of Common Gateway Interface (CGI) binaries in the C programming language and came up with the first version of PHP.

PHP is an open source server side scripting language used for creating dynamic web pages. Open source means computer programs that are publicly owned, so they are basically free. PHP was also intended to replace Perl scripts to make creating dynamic web pages easier on the server side.

Originally, PHP stood for Personal Home Page before it was changed to mean Hypertext Preprocessor; and it was the beginning of dynamic web pages that could be processed on the server side.

At the same time, JavaScript was being developed by Sun Microsystems for the Navigator Netscape browser as a client side script that could also process dynamic web pages.

As you can see, these are really just programs that were developed to produce functions like drop-down menus and interactive forms that would look the same on every browser. Also, whenever you hear about JavaScript and Jscript, you will usually hear the similar VBScript mentioned along with Dynamic HTML (or DHTML) as well as the AJAX framework. Again, it's up to you to decide what kind of coding and software you want to use.

Active Server Pages (ASP) is another part of the evolution of dynamic web pages. The first thing that you have to understand about ASP, is that it works along with the Information Internet Server (the Windows operating system), ASP.NET, and FrontPage; which are all Microsoft products that were developed as Microsoft Windows made its move to increase its product line for the Internet.

These Microsoft products were developed from the same existing open source software as the others, but built so that the average user could develop dynamic web pages without learning as much computer code or scripting languages.

If you are still confused, don't let it bother you. Suffice it to say that whenever you develop a web site, you're going to meet some know-it-all who is going to be tossing around all kinds of terms. So don't let them throw you.

When it come to creating dynamic web pages , remember that these products are nothing more than different options, and whatever software you ultimately use to create a website is largely a matter of preference.

Chapter Eight

A database driven website has *many benefits*.

Another way to build your website and increase its capacity for successful Internet Marketing is to create a database driven web site. This would be in addition to coding your site with HTML, but is well worth learning how to do in the long run. A database driven website will not only allow you to take advantage of the unique benefits of Internet marketing, but will also make your website easier to manage if you are developing a website on your own.

In order to understand the way a database driven website works, you have to think about the two functioning parts of a live website – the client side, and the server side. The client side of your web site is anything on your website that a browser will allow a viewer to see or do while they are online. For example, one thing that a viewer may be allowed to do while they are on your website is fill out a form to be on your mailing list - because the form is available on the client side. What they will not be allowed to do is view your entire mailing list, because this is stored on the server side and the viewer does not have access to it.

The server side of your website is made up any files or information that is stored on the server (computer) at your hosting company. The viewer's browser (client side) is there to act as an interpreter to show the viewer the web pages that you want them to see from the server side of your website. It is wise to use HTML, PHP, and other scripting languages when you develop your website.

A Data Base Driven Website Will Build a Strong Customer Base

Creating a database driven website is the process of storing and updating information on the server side, which will later be viewed on the client side. To put it very simply, you will be storing information and content for your web pages in the data bases you create on your server. This will allow you to accomplish two important tasks.

First, you can embed code into your web pages that will create interactive forms for the viewer. This will allow the viewer to input information into the web pages that you can use later - like names, addresses, and in the case of sales – credit card information.

Second, your data bases can also hold content for your web pages which you can import to your web pages so that they will constantly have fresh content. Having this kind of capabilities on your website will really boost your Internet marketing efforts.

This will make it easier for any browser to interpret your web pages for several reasons. This is because these scripting languages help the browser present your website authentically to more viewers, which in turn can increase the possibility for more sales. If you use What-You-See-Is-What-You-Get website software (software with built-in coding such as FrontPage or Dreamweaver), you are taking your chances with regards to how your website will look on different browsers and also to the search engines.

In actuality, browsers are much more uniform these days, but there are other reasons to use server side scripting to produce dynamic results on the server side; the main reason being is the ability to develop a database driven website.

There are many free scripting tools to help you manage your web pages on your server so that viewers can input information into your dynamic forms in order to be stored on the server for later use, and also for you to create fresh content for your website. This is why server side scripting was invented.

The first thing to do is to create a database on your server in MySQL. (MySQL is a database associated with dynamic web pages and generally comes with most cheap web hosting packages.) This database can contain content, customer messages, or anything else that you want to put in the pages of your website. You will also have a separate database to collect information from your customers.

Then, you will create a template for each of your web pages for the information you want to display or collect. This template will make up the content of each page, which will consist of your HTML tag, the title, and the body of the page. The great thing about having a template for each web page is that in the case of creating new content for your web pages, you can change the content of the page by importing new content from the databases into the title or the body of your content without having to recode the page itself.

Even if you do buy new content or hire a writer, there isn't any need to recode the content. All you have to do is put the new content in the database and connect it to the page. The page with the new content will be generated on the server side when someone views the page.

Getting Started With a Database Driven Website

To get it all started, all you have to do is connect the database on the server to the web pages where you either want to display or collect information. A database connection is simply a function that lets your web pages connect with your data base through server side scripting. Using PHP and MySQL together is the best way to accomplish this.

PHP and MySQL combined together open up a lot of other possibilities when it comes to creating and processing dynamic web pages and creating a customer database. The fact that PHP can be used to create forms for your customers and keep their information for retrieval helps out with customer service because you can set up your MySQL database to retain all of the information about someone who visits your web site. This way, you can give every customer a code and associate that code with all of the cells of information in the database that pertain to them - like their address, phone number, or a buying history, and also give them the option to update that information right on the website.

So, if their address changes they can update it themselves without having to send you an email. As well, you can update something like the status of an order in the data base that the customer can retrieve through a form on the site. So you can both check for new information in real time without having to exchange emails. You can also use the data base to create cookies that will personally greet the viewer when they log on. This information can be further used to create email lists for Internet marketing purposes.

A data base driven web site does a lot of work guiding both new and current customers through their purchase, right up to the automatic shipping.

For a new customer, an account can be automatically created, and for an existing customer, a query can be run on the data base to get account information. The order is taken, the stock is pulled, and the item shipped automatically.

Through the whole process, there are prompts for every action the customer has to take. If there are any problems, the customer will get an automatic email with the details. Making the purchase easy for the customers is truly important to get the sale on the Internet. With a database driven website, you give the customer one more reason to buy right away.

Chapter Nine

A database driven website helps with *email campaigns*.

With a database driven website, one of the biggest things that you can do is start an email campaign that targets the niche market that you want to reach. If someone visits your website, they don't have to buy anything, they just have to sign up for your email list to be included in on any special offers that you want to send out to preferred customers.

An email campaign is only second to search engine optimization when it comes to being able to track marketing results. This is because it is completely traceable with regards to who you are contacting, what they are purchasing and how much they will buy in response to your marketing efforts.

Make Your Email Campaign More Successful

With a database driven website, you can track each buyer with codes like these:

- Past purchases
- Initial purchases
- Special offer purchases
- Discount purchases
- Seasonal purchases
- Affiliate marketing purchases
- Wholesale purchases

The list goes on, but with a database driven website, you have a much better understanding of what you need to do to increase sales at any given time.

Managing Your Email List Will Increase Sales

Another great advantage about a database driven website and email campaigns is that customers can also unsubscribe at any time. You can also send an automatic email letting them know that you will protect their privacy and stop sending them offers.

That's the kind of customer service that will keep your customers loyal and actually have them refer more people to you. Always remember, a good referral is always worth more than trying to trick someone into making a one-time purchase.

You'll get a lot more mileage out of an email list that you manage than one that you buy from an email company.

Outsourced email lists are often outdated and are aimed to try and trick people into responding to them. Do you really want to run a business where you write a fake subject title to entice someone into responding? Here's why that doesn't work:

The response rate to an email list is one percent to three percent. That is in the best case scenario, where you are counting on reaching the right target group to open an email and think, "I was caught at the right exact moment when I wanted to purchase that exact item. It's a good thing that I have my credit card handy."

Take a moment and think about how you delete your own email and you can imagine how quickly your unsolicited email will be sent to the recycle bin on someone else's computer. Also, many people make up temporary email addresses just for junk email and then abandon them without even reading the junk emails.

While it is unusual for anyone to open junk emails, many people will at least consider looking at an email from a company where they have done business with or at least requested to be on an email list.

True Story: Working as a freelance writer, so many people have asked me to write sales letters so they can send them out as emails.

I finally agreed to write a set of sales letters, and it turned out that the buyer was unhappy with my work. (There were actually twenty keywords in each letter they wanted written.) I have never written sales letters for anyone again because I finally realized what companies are looking for in a sales letter.

They want a magic sales letter that is so powerful it will actually induce the buyer to make a purchase upon reading it.

This sales tactic is known by the term **sales conversion.** However, if you are looking for that perfectly worded, long-winded sales letter, I am here to tell you that unfortunately, it doesn't exist. Today's consumer is way too sophisticated to be so moved by any sales letter that they are going to buy your product after reading it.

A much more effective approach is to present your information as quickly as possible on a website so the reader knows exactly what you are selling. There is no way you are going to stop them from going to at least five different sites before they make a decision.

That's the whole point of Internet Marketing. In the end, however, it is all about niche marketing; and the company that will make the most sales is the person who gives the clearest and most compelling information on their product as quickly as possible and then has the right price and customer service for that product.

Chapter Ten

Ecommerce components are an important part of *Internet marketing.*

Ecommerce is fascinating in the fact that it can help anyone realize the dream of owning their own business, without having the enormous burden of the traditional start-up costs associated with a brick and mortar store. In fact, it's one of the few business ventures where you can take a small investment and launch an international enterprise - almost in an afternoon. This kind of unlimited opportunity is the stuff that dreams are made of for many entrepreneurs; in fact, just the thought of almost effortlessly opening an international storefront where the whole world can shop is enough to get even the most cynical among us to start imagining how much money we can make.

However, the reality of any business is not that simple. Just like any other successful business, the secret to ecommerce success is in the details, and even more so in the technology. Ecommerce web hosting can become a technical and strategic nightmare if you don't understand the mechanics of how online sales technology works.

Specifically, credit card processing problems can be a permanent setback that will put you out of business if you don't do your home work.

Anyone in marketing will tell you that successful marketing means lots of sales, and also that making sales means closing the sale. In the case of Internet marketing, closing the sale is done at the shopping cart on your web site, so it is imperative to make sure that is always working properly.

Remember, if people don't have confidence in the technical and security aspects of your website, they aren't going to hand over their credit card. So the traffic that you have worked so hard to get to your site will inevitably give their money to someone else. As well, the mishandling of credit card numbers can lead to charges of fraud, which can also put an end to your business and possibly land you in jail.

What Technical Elements are needed for Successful Ecommerce?

There are many different technical elements that go into building and managing an ecommerce site which many web hosting companies and web developers tend to gloss over when they are selling you their product.

One of the biggest ones is taking credit cards. This is surprising, because while marketing means sales, a sale really only counts if you get paid. So, to reiterate: Closing the sale is an essential part of Internet Marketing, which means having a secure, easy-to-use shopping cart where your customer will feel confident to pay you for your goods and services.

Ecommerce sites are complicated. Creating a professional looking site and getting traffic is hard enough, but you also have to look trustworthy enough to get customers to actually give you their credit card number in order to make a sale.

To make this task more difficult, shoppers will compare your site to major retailers who have unlimited resources to spend on their websites; so the competition can make your website look amateurish.

However, with a fluidly operating credit card processor, you shouldn't have a problem making sales from the people who visit your web site and want to buy your product. On the technical end, this means that the shopping cart and the credit card processing absolutely have to work right. This because customers may be forgiving when it comes to how expert your site looks, but they won't give a credit card number to someone they don't trust.

To break it down, you will need to consider four technical elements:

- A Shopping Cart
- A Payment Gateway
- An SSL Certificate
- A Merchant Account

If you sign up for a web hosting package, it will probably include a shopping cart and possibly a shared SSL certificate, but not a payment gateway, and definitely not a merchant account. To get started, let's look at the easiest part of this formula, which is the shopping cart.

The Shopping Cart:

A shopping cart is the icon on your website where people can drop the items they want to purchase during an Internet shopping session. The shopping cart will keep a list of the items and add up how much they cost.

You can also customize your shopping cart to do other things like calculate coupons, give quantity discounts, add shipping and handling, and provide other services that you might find at the checkout in a traditional brick and mortar store. The shopping cart can be located anywhere on you website but needs to be accessible at all times. This is an important technical aspect of Internet marketing.

Setting up a shopping cart is the easiest part of an ecommerce site because most of them are free and part of open source software packages. They also come ready-to-go with your free sitebuilder if you sign up for web hosting plan; so even if you don't know anything about ecommerce, you can set up and modify a shopping cart easily.

The most popular carts are Zen carts, Agora carts, and OS Commerce carts, but whatever cart you want to use is a matter of preference; and since they are basically free, you can change your shopping cart if you find that you like another one better.

The Payment Gateway:

Once your customer is ready to commit to the sale and check out, they need to give you some form of payment, which is generally by credit card or an electronic payment like Pay Pal. This is where the payment gateway comes into play.

The payment gateway is actually a paid service that sends out the customer's credit card information and gets it approved for payment. It is accessed by your customer when they hit the 'submit order' button that you have created on your web site. This is also the go-between that connects your web site to your merchant account.

Without it, you can't process credit cards and deposit the funds into your bank account. If you use a payment gateway like PayPal, this service may be combined with your SSL certificate, which you also need in order to take credit cards.

The SSL Certificate:

The SSL certificate is the security part of your ecommerce web site and you may have to pay separately for this service. This may be in addition to the percentage of sales from your merchant account, and the fee for your payment gateway.

An SSL (Secure Sockets Layer) certificate or TLS (Transport Layer Security) is an encryption protocol that keeps information that you trade on the Internet secure. This is mainly to prevent someone from hacking credit card information from your transactions.

When you sign up for a hosting plan with a web hosting company, you will sometimes get a shared SSL certificate, but it doesn't necessarily have anything to do with the security of credit cards that you accept.

It may just mean that the server where your web files are located is secure, and the SSL certificate verifies that your URL (Domain Name) is part of that server. So, the shared SSL certificate that is free may have more to do with the fact that you can verify that there is security on the server where your web site is located, than it does with being able to process secure credit card transactions.

Banks are more concerned about safely transferring credit card data securely over the Internet from your website to the credit card processor, and then to your bank account. This is because unless it is encrypted, this information can be intercepted by hackers. This is especially true when it is transmitted over wireless networks.

In the case of buying a web hosting package, find out what the shared SSL certificate covers. If it includes the secure transfer of credit card information and a payment gateway that can be used to connect your website to your merchant account at your bank, great!

However, make sure to get all of the details. If it doesn't, you will have to buy the payment gateway and SSL certificate separately from your hosting account. This can be expensive, but is necessary to encrypt credit card information before you send it out over the Internet. The general rule is a 128 bit to a 256 bit encryption code, which is what most credit card processors use.

Some banks will request this information when you sign up for a merchant account and some will provide this service to you. It all depends on where you go. In order to get security for the transfer of credit card information, you may have to sign up for a service like VeriSign, Authorize.Net, PayPal, or another authorization service that you can find that will process your credit card payments and deposit them into your merchant account.

Most people who are new to ecommerce and sign up for an all-inclusive web hosting account get upset when they realize that there is more to taking credit cards than just paying the monthly web hosting fee that is charged by the web hosting company. This is generally because the web hosting packages are often advertised as 'ecommerce ready' which is correct to a certain extent, but can still be a misleading phrase to use.

The Merchant Account:

Once you have a shopping cart set up and a secure credit card processor, you will have to set up a merchant account with a bank.

A merchant account with a bank is simply a deposit account that observes the rules for deposit as set forth by MasterCard and Visa. If you want to accept American Express and Discover Card, you will have to contact them separately.

When you set up a merchant account, you will have to sign a contract. Be careful when you sign a contract with a bank because they will abide by the contract with no exceptions. The contract may be for a certain amount of years, and you will have to pay some sort of transactions fees and probably a monthly fee that will all be spelled out in the contract that you sign with your merchant account holder.

Transaction fees may be priced per transaction or as a percentage of the transaction, like one percent of the gross sale. Always shop around for the best deal, and be aware that you are personally responsible for the merchant account - so if your credit is bad you may be charged a higher transaction rate.

You are also responsible for the fact that if you have a chargeback from a customer who was not happy with their product and that you failed to resolve the issue, the amount will be subtracted from your account and you will be responsible for the funds.

As well, if you are found to be committing credit card fraud - including numbers being stolen from your site and charged on illegally, you can also be required to pay back the fraudulent charges. This is the reason why you need to be careful about the validity of your SSL certificate.

Further Credit card Security:

Remember, there are also security issues on your web hosting site as well. You should never, ever store credit card numbers on your server. If you need to keep them for reference, they should be stored in a file on a computer that no one has access to. If you have a shared hosting plan, you have to be extra careful when it comes to security, because anyone who shares your server can start hacking into other web sites if they have enough time on their hands and they know what they are doing.

As well, sometimes shopping carts have security issues, which you should read up on before you decide which shopping cart you are going to use. When you let people shop with you, you will have their shipping address, phone number, and banking information all in the same place. This is a big responsibility, and one which you will be held responsible for if there is a case of identity theft and the victim or the state decides to press charges.

Once you have everything in place - the shopping cart, merchant account, and payment gateway/SSL certificate, this should have you up and running and able to accept payments on your ecommerce web site. It's probably better to start with a simple shopping cart to see how it works before you try anything complicated. Also, don't forget to test your check-out system every day to make sure the entire credit card process is working. Any down time with your shopping cart or credit card processing will cost you sales.

A Few Other Technical Aspects to Think About:

- Make sure that your website prompts the buyer's next action.
- Assume that even the most sophisticated buyer has no time to think about why your ecommerce site is not ready for them to buy.
- Don't let your website's technology delay the buyer's final decision to buy.
- The more you protect the mechanisms of the buying process, the less sales you will lose to indecision.

True story: When I go shopping on the Internet, before I even consider buying anything, there are a few things I look for on a web site. That's a security icon, a 1-800 number and a return policy. If I don't see these items clearly displayed, I go somewhere else to buy.

That's just me, but you should always think about what would make you and your customers buy from a website. If you need to see a security icon on a website before you buy, chances are your customer may want to see one too. You have to go that extra mile to make sure that your site has the technical features that your customer will need to see to feel comfortable shopping in order to maximize your sales.

Chapter Eleven

Learning SEO makes all of the *difference.*

Search Engine Optimization is the next step in achieving authentic Internet marketing. Search Engine optimization will further build on your existing organic marketing efforts to increase traffic, raise your rankings, increase sales, and help you build a sustainable presence on the Internet.

Like advertising, however, it is not something that you can just pay for and expect any results.

When advertising doesn't work to increase Internet sales, search engine optimization is the next thing that people turn to increase profits. There are just as many companies that sell search engine optimization as advertising, and they can't wait to talk to you.

They throw around terms like keyword density, latent semantic indexing, algorithms, ranking reports, back links, black hat, article directories, content, Meta tags, etc., (and a lot of other theories that they promise that will get you ahead of everyone else) but what are they really talking about?

These SEO companies are talking about increasing your rankings temporarily though search engine optimization tactics. *Tactics* is the key word here, because just like pay-per-click advertising, thousands of more eyes will see your product through the search engines; but the question still remains, *"Who is going to buy it?"*

So you have to ask yourself, *"What good will this do my company?"* The answer to that question is that as long as you pay your SEO Company they will get you traffic and rankings. That's fine, but what about sales? If you read a contract from any SEO company, the only thing that is promised to you is higher rankings, and increased traffic through links and content.

Website Content is More Important than You Might Think

The next question to ask is, "Who is writing content for me and what is being linked to me?" The answer here is - *nobody and nothing* – this is the reason why search engine optimization strategies and tactics don't work for any longer that what you pay for them.

Like authentic Internet marketing, organic search engine optimization will only complement what you are already doing; and you can actually do it yourself much better than anyone else. This is because you are the only person that knows your company the best. So who better to work on your search engine optimization than you?

Learning the basics of organic search engine optimization will help you more than paying someone else to do it for you. You will get more traffic to your site, get your website ranked higher, and make your site more relevant on a permanent basis.

The term 'search engine optimization' is self-explanatory. It means to optimize your website for search engines so that they will rank your site higher. SEO companies are companies that make money by being on top of what the search engines are looking for when they hand out rankings, but this is backwards thinking.

This is because the only thing that the search engines are looking for is a way to organize information by importance so that people can find it easier. So if you circumvent the system by tricking the search engines, you will always have to be paying someone for rankings and advertising.

The search engines clear out all of the fake content and links from the ranking about every two weeks, which is why you have to pay for advertising and SEO companies every month if you want to keep these kinds of rankings. You can only stop this cycle by developing your own importance and relevance on the Internet.

Search engine optimization came about as a way to organize websites on the Internet so that people could find them by order of importance. Since most things, including opinions, are for sale on the Internet, it naturally became organized like a big shopping mall. Searching for information is like going through a mall directory - you type in what you are looking for in a search box and the directory will tell you the most likely place to find it. "What you are looking for" is the easiest way to describe the term 'keyword', which is what search engine optimization is built around.

For example, if you are looking for 'linens' you will naturally want to find the store with the most selection of linens, or the store that is an expert on linens. The search engines will find the store with the most linens or the linen expert - based on the web site with the most written about linens.

Search engines can't see pictures, only text; so the website that has the most written about linens and has also optimized their writing so that the search engines will determine that this is the foremost authority on linens will be ranked number one in your search, and so on down the line.

Using this logic, the search engines will probably come up with a department store, but you can narrow your linens search by using the keyword 'bed sheets'. You may get a linens store from that keyword, but you can narrow your search even further by searching for 'cotton bed sheets', 'Egyptian cotton bed sheets', and then finally 'discount 3000 thread count Egyptian cotton bed sheets.'

You can also narrow the name by manufacturer and color until you find exactly what you are looking for. 'What you are looking for' is what makes keywords so important and what makes the entire Internet work.

Of course, in a free market, you can see how people would immediately take advantage of this situation. If you want to be ranked number one for cotton sheets, you keyword stuff your website with the keyword 'cotton sheets' and the search engines will rank you number one. Sites like this are quickly banned or penalized, and if an SEO company is selling on a high keyword density strategy, don't buy it.

So, what do Search Engines Want?

Now, what pleases the search engines most is called organic SEO, which means that you build your rankings naturally, by authentically becoming an authority on the products you sell, or the information you distribute, and that is what we are talking about here.

Content is the next step in search engine optimization. Content is meaningful and relevant text that is written around your keywords. It is then posted on your web site using HTML and Meta tags so that the search engines can find it. The search engines do not recognize graphics and flash as content, and so these elements will not get you any rankings whatsoever.

What you need on your website is keyword-rich content in order to get the rankings that you want on the Internet. This is because the only way that someone is going to find your web site when they do a search for your product is if the keywords for your product appear in the content on your site. For example, if someone is looking for cotton sheets and that is what you sell, the keyword 'cotton sheets' is a keyword that needs to appear in the content on your web site.

Your site can also get higher rankings though a process known as 'linking.' Finding and ranking your site through keywords isn't the only way that search engines and others can find your web site. They can also do it by your links to other sites. This can be accomplished in several different ways.

First, you can write articles and submit them to article submissions directories that will publish your article along with what is called a 'back link' to your web site. Back links, or inbound links are the best kind to get, because the search engines automatically assume that if other sites have linked to you, that you are the authority for that keyword. This means that they will give you a higher ranking over other web sites.

The other kinds of links you can have are reciprocal links, where a web site with similar content will share a link with you to generate more traffic for both sites.

Those are the basics of search engine optimization, which includes key words, content, HTML/Meta tags, and links; all of which are used to get higher rankings on the Internet. This is all an important part of an Internet marketing campaign, and also something that will work better if you are directly involved in the process.

True story: Working in the writing department for an SEO company was an eye opening experience.

It was an okay company, and the clients got the promised rankings, but they always left after three months. At first, I couldn't figure it out. The rankings were delivered as promised, so why leave?

And then I realized what was wrong. Our services only got rankings as long as we were all working full time on the account. There was no permanency to what we were doing.

Why? The content was generic, the links were bad, and there was some kind of automated system that was making it all work. Our services may have improved rankings, but they didn't improve sales because there was nothing authentic about what we were doing. When the client left, their ranking immediately plummeted, and essentially they had spent their money for nothing. We were always being laid off as clients left; and after a year of that, I left, too.

The Condensed Book of Internet Marketing

Chapter Twelve

Keywords tell the *whole story.*

More time and effort is spent on explaining how keywords will help your website than is necessary, and yet, there are an incredible amount of keyword research services and experts that you can pay a lot of money to in order to find those keywords that will give you the highest rankings.

Even better, after all of reading all of those articles about keywords and the money spent paying for keyword research, many business owners will still walk away, saying "I could have done that!"

And you know what? That's because they might have been able to do just that. Finding the right keywords and using them to increase traffic to your sight is the most over-rated task, and can actually be the easiest one to accomplish.

Why Keyword Research is Easy

Keywords are the biggest part of search engine optimization because while the Internet is organized like a shopping mall, it is also organized like a card catalogue. This is a statement meaning, that while web pages are organized by popularity; they are also organized by subject.

Think about yourself going to the library, knowing the subject that you want to look up, but not knowing the title of any books. That's exactly how the Internet works. If you want to find a website about the history of dogs, you'll type the word 'dog' into a search engine dialogue box. To narrow it down, you can type in 'the history of beagles' or the 'history of beagles in Massachusetts", and so on.

As part of a successful Internet marketing campaign, all you have to do is make sure that all of those words are included, organized and marked for the search engines. That's all there is to it.

If you have ever noticed that while conducting a personal search on the Internet that sometimes when you search for a keyword like 'beagle' and unrelated sites pop up on your search like 'homes for sale' and 'lose weight now', you can see that someone has paid a service to find any keyword possibly related to the word 'beagle' in an attempt to expose their site to absolutely anyone they can in the hopes that they will buy something.

Get Keywords That are Related to What You are Selling

Ask yourself – do you make it a habit of clicking on those unrelated search results, or do you get angry that you can't find the information or product you are looking for?

So why would you pay someone all of that money to put your web site all over the Internet when no one is going to respond or may even get annoyed at you?

Or, as a beagle breeder, would you like your website to appear in the same searches as people looking for weight loss and a new home? Is there a significant and expanding group of people that have a love for beagles, a need for a new home and a desire for weight loss in common? Maybe, but are they your target market? Probably not.

The fact is, you can come up with all of the keywords you need in a few hours, by yourself, and you can check their accuracy for free on the Internet.

For example, if you sell hair care products, you are first going to want to come up with all of the keywords that make up a hair care product line like: shampoo, conditioner, hair spray, hair gel, hair mousse, repair serum, cream rinse, pomade, hair tonic, etc.

These keywords will simply be all of the products that you sell and any related products that you may sell at a later date, or even key words that will let you link to a similar site.

So just because you don't sell something, doesn't mean you can't use the keyword- as long as it is related to what you are selling –like the keyword 'hair dryer.' That's because in this case, while someone may be looking for a new hair dryer, it's more than likely that they are also looking for hair conditioner as well - because maybe their old hair dryer damaged their hair.

So if you include the keyword hair dryer as a related product, even though you don't sell them, you have a person who will come across your website when they weren't looking for it, and possible buy your product.

Those are related keywords, and the search engines will be looking for them on your website and in your content. This is what SEO people mean when they talk about latent semantic indexing. It's another more human way that search engines rank your site.

In other words, you can't just mention shampoo a hundred times and expect to get rankings. You actually have to mention all of the keywords that go with it in order for the search engines to deem your website as an authority and give it a high ranking.

You Need to Really Brainstorm in Order to Come up with Relevant Keywords

Some relevant keywords for hair care products might be hair dryer, curling iron, diffuser, barrettes, hair bands, scrunchies, combs, brushes, curlers, hair color, hair style, split ends, hair cut, frizz, tint, dye, teased, extensions, perms, roots, follicle, scalp, straightener, braids, afro, weave, wig, etc.

Other key words will include brand manes. Brand names are important to have on your site because search engines can find them too.

However, besides your content, the best place to have brand names is underneath the image of your product, because while search engines can't find pictures, they can find brand names in product descriptions. If someone searches for a specific product and there is a picture attached, the search engine will bring up the product description, the product shot, the price, and a link to your website. This is like an instant sale.

A keyword mistake that many people make is to try to rank for a word like 'shampoo.' There are two reasons why this doesn't work.

First of all, every single company on the Internet that sells hair care products is trying to rank number one for that word. There is no chance that you are ever going to get it - and if you do, you won't keep it for long.

Secondly, potential customers don't just type in shampoo and expect to see something they are going to buy. Internet surfers are way too savvy for that now. Instead, they will either type in the brand name of a shampoo they want; or, if they don't know the type of shampoo they want, they will start a search for their particular needs. So if someone has damaged hair, they may use the keywords 'dry hair treatment.'

This is extremely important to understand because this is where you will get people who are specifically looking for your product. So not only do you have to keywords, you also have to have keyword phrases that customers will enter into a search.

In the case of hair products, you can go even further and use related words like dry, oily, damaged, burnt, over-processed, thinning, healthy, tangled, long, short, spiky, curly, straight, red, black, brown, blonde, shimmery, highlighted, unruly, flat, thick, wavy, and any other word you can think of to describe hair.

To combine everything together, you can come up with a title for a web page that a search engine will not only recognize as meaningful and relevant, but will pull up in a keyword search as a website where people with dry, damaged hair can get help.

Here is what a sample title for a hair care products web page might look like: 'Herbal Care's new deep conditioning shampoo gets out tangles, and repairs dry damaged hair caused by your hair dryer.'

It's simple really, but someone can find this web page by the brand name or the keywords 'dry hair', 'damaged hair', 'dry damaged hair', 'deep conditioning' or 'deep conditioning, dry damaged hair', etc.

Now realistically, these are keywords that people are looking for when they surf the Internet. A good keyword strategy is to think of a problem that your product solves and use those related keywords along with your related keywords and descriptive keywords.

Regional Keywords Will Narrow Down a Search Even More

As well, if you have a service that is regional, like a plumbing service, it is important to include keywords that pertain to your location. This can include countries, states, counties, cities, regions, neighborhoods, street names, zip codes, area codes, shopping centers, etc.

Here is an example for the title of a regional service: 'Smith's Plumbing Provides Emergency Plumbing Service for Flooded Basements in the Pine Valley Area." When you have a regional business, you should definitely take advantage of niche marketing on the Internet.

This sounds like a magical formula, but it isn't. You just have to think about what someone would want to know, or the problem they would want to solve and then assign keywords to it. However, be careful not to go overboard.

Keyword density is important as well. Just like in a real conversation, search engines don't like if you use keywords too much. Just like you tune someone out in a conversation, the search engines will drop your rankings if you use keywords in an unnatural way. When you use keywords over abundantly, it's called spamming or keyword-stuffing, and spamming can get you banned from the Internet. This is an old ploy used by people trying to trick the search engines into thinking they are an authority on a subject to get rakings.

If you have a real product and real information, you don't have to do that. Just talk normally and use a normal keyword density. A normal keyword density is about 2% of your total word count. To figure out your keyword density, simply divide the number of keywords by the number of total words in the body of your text.

For example, if your content has 500 words and you mention your keyword ten times, you have a keyword density of 2%. That is more than enough for the search engines to count your article as being relevant to the keyword.

To check your work and get more ideas and statistics about keywords, there are free web sites that you can go to find keywords that are relevant to your product and how they are ranked. Chances are you will find most of the words you have already chosen and some others that didn't occur to you.

Remember that this information, including how many people are searching for these key words is all free. Any keyword research service that charges a fee will give you similar, if not exactly, the same results. To find out about free keywords, just do a search.

Always check out the keywords your competition uses.

To get even more keywords from your competition, do a keyword search for words you think you should be using and go to each competitor's website. If you right click anywhere on the homepage, a menu will usually pop up. Scroll down to **view source** and click on it. The HTML code, including the keywords for the website will normally pop up. You can get all kinds of information like keywords and other phrases that similar companies in your industry use.

True Story: Working as a writer for an SEO company, I was sometimes waiting for the keyword analyst to come up with the keywords so I could start writing content.

He was hailed as a real guru, deeply searching the Internet for keywords specifically aimed at helping each individual client. This was an import part of our SEO service, and charged for accordingly.

One day while I got tired of waiting and took out a sheet of note book paper and wrote down the keywords that any logical person would mention if they were talking about this product.

This was before I even knew that free keyword websites existed. I got 75% of the keywords right. I'm not knocking the service that the company gave because the keyword researcher was experience and seemed to know what he was doing.

What I'm saying is with your own imagination, common sense, and some help from the free keyword sites on the Internet, you can do keyword research yourself. And if you're wrong about a few words, is it really worth paying an SEO company for a job that you can do 95% accurately yourself?

Chapter Thirteen

Writing content for SEO *isn't as hard as you think.*

Content writing is a crucial part of Internet marketing, but not every business owner has much of an interest in doing it themselves.

However, the main difference between mass Internet marketing and authentic Internet marketing is the personal touch that you add to the whole marketing campaign; which, in the case of Internet marketing, means a lot of written communication.

This personal, written communication is the very foundation of authentic Internet marketing because it addresses the problem of the ever-fragmenting mass media.

While you can still use the Internet, radio, television, and newspapers to reach huge amounts of people, there are so many options where people can get product information that they trust, that no one medium is dominating.

The Internet is just one other place to see what's going on in the world. So keep in mind that the Internet is not your new chance to address the masses to get mass sales; rather it is a quicker way to find the people that you want to sell to and get them to buy right away.

This is why it is important to address your writing to one single person. Ultimately, only one person will be reading your message as they sit at their computer. You have their complete attention. So doesn't it make sense to talk to that one person?

When it Comes to Niche Marketing, Only Talk to One Person

When you write, imagine that you are talking to a relative or friend. This will make your writing more realistic and make your customer feel like you are there for them. It will make them want to buy from someone who knows them.

If you dread writing, there are many ways to get around it, mainly by paying someone else to do it. This is the easiest way to get the job done and work on the part of your business that you think is really important, but you will find that proficient Internet writers are expensive and in high demand.

On the other hand, really poor writing is cheap and unreliable; so what other choice do you have? The answer is to do it yourself. Writing your own content is the best way to get your own ideas across and create more sales. It may sound like a lot of work, but just like it is easy to reach so many people on the Internet, it is also easy to write a lot of content yourself.

This is because you already have all of your main keywords, your related keywords and keyword phrases to get you started. So you aren't exactly looking at a blank page.

If you have a product or a message and have a reason why you are selling it, you already have an idea of what to say. Now, here's the good part. There is also a format for everything that you write on the Internet when you are selling a product - and guess what? Everything you write for the Internet is short, simple, and to-the-point.

This means that you can turn out content on a daily basis without an excruciating amount of effort. There are even tools to help turn your original content into variations that you can also put out there if you need mass- produced content.

When you write for the Internet with the idea of selling a product, there are an unlimited amount of places where you can write, but the types of places where you can write break-down into these main categories:

- Your own web pages
- Articles Directories
- Blogs
- Social Networks
- Emails
- Newsletters
- Chat Rooms

Each venue has its own restrictions, but they can all be written quickly, because they are meant to get the word out about your website and your product - not burden someone with something like a Master's dissertation.

People don't have time for that. On the Internet, everyone likes to look at all kinds of things; so they want to glance at what you have written, get the idea, and look at your website to see if it's interesting. Then they move on to another site.

So if you don't like writing long diatribes, this is a great relief. However, it's still better to write these bits and pieces yourself, because like-minded people will want to see more of what you have to say, and others that aren't in the market to buy can move on to something more entertaining.

Personalized, authentic writing is the best way to entice potential buyers who are in your niche market to come look at your product.

It would be nice to sell to everyone on the Internet, but that would be impossible. The sales strategy here is to attract the people in your niche market (the people who are going to buy) with pieces of information that will arouse their interest and get them to click over to your website.

Since this all occurs in a matter of seconds, it pays to be brief and get right to the point when you write. The format of writing for the Internet is extremely simple, and actually dates back to high school English classes:

- Every paragraph should have a topic sentence
- Every paragraph should only have one idea.
- Every sentence in the paragraph should back up the topic sentence.
- Paragraphs are four sentences maximum.
- Sentences are only ten words maximum.
- Articles are only three to five paragraphs maximum. (300-500 words)
- Grammar and spelling must be perfect. (Search engines may not have enough artificial intelligence to appreciate good writing, but they can pick up on bad grammar and will give you bad marks for it.)

Here's Something Else to Consider

When it comes to Internet writing, the main key word must be in the first sentence of the body; and all related keywords have to be in the first 100 to 250 words of the text.

This confirms that the article is really about what the title suggests, and also goes with the organized composition rules that high school English teachers try to teach. As well, search engines may not always use Meta tags, so don't rely on them to make up for your own lack of relevance.

That's it. It looks simple, but these rules make sense because people are only glancing not reading; and they won't be able to comprehend anything more than simple ideas. Accordingly, everything is also written to be very short. This is because you are only writing just enough to get the attention of the right people and have them take action on your ideas.

True Story: When I worked for the SEO Company, what I realized was it didn't matter how intellectual your writing was. You just had to do it on a daily basis.

Most customers get used to instant communication and they start to worry when someone isn't always available. As a business owner or a marketing director, you can circumvent a lot of customer unrest simply by putting out articles every day.

Even if you can't do that, you can blog to keep customers up-to-date on your company's activities. It takes a lot less time to keep people informed as you have new products and information than it does to do damage control.

Chapter Fourteen

Internet marketing has a *writing strategy*.

Of course, you want to combine this style of writing with a marketing strategy, because that is what is going to intrigue potential customers.

There is a sample marketing strategy that has been around for a long time. Since you are only dealing with four or five paragraphs, an authentic marketing strategy can be easily broken down into a simple outline.

- **Identify a problem**
- **Identify who has the problem**
- **Identify an emotional benefit**
- **Prompt a response**

This sales strategy is perfect for getting people to buy on the Internet, which, in marketing terms, is looked upon as a **call to action**. However, the writing has to be subtle. This is because you can't persuade or pressure someone into buying a product like you can on the phone or in a face-to-face sales pitch.

For example, in the case of a flat rate mortgage, you will want to appeal to someone who may not have great credit, but has a longtime job and wants to start over with their life. The problem is identified, but then you have to think about who your customer actually is.

Is this someone who has bad credit, someone who has relocated with a new job, or someone who has their first job out of college? All of these potential borrowers may fit the profile, but who are you really targeting? As a potential Internet marketer, this is something that is important if you want to make sales.

An emotional benefit is important as well. In the case of mortgage brokers, the emotional benefit is that everyone in the United States wants to own their own home. The emotional benefit in this case is financial security and the peace of mind that you have an affordable investment that also builds equity.

Once you have written about an emotional benefit - prompting a response, getting a call to action, getting a sales conversion, or whatever you want to call it, is easy. Once you have established that you are not only an authority, but that you also care about the people you sell to, they will start buying.

Now, let's see what this kind of writing looks like in three different Internet formats:

1. **A homepage**

2. **An article submission**

3. **A blog**

These examples are written in *plain text* for a mortgage broker:

Example 1: Plain Text Content for the Home page of a Mortgage Broker

Worldwide Lending Group –Home of the Flat Rate Mortgage
It's a great time to buy real estate!

At Worldwide Lending Group, we specialize in getting first time buyers a flat rate mortgage at a rate they can afford! We will find the right flat rate mortgage for you!

We offer:

•Free Assessment of Your Financial Situation
•Free Assistance with all Loan Application
•Help with Closing Costs
•Largest Assortment of Mortgage Products
•Direct Relationships with Major Lenders

Are you afraid that you won't get a suitable flat rate mortgage because you are a first time buyer?

Now is a great time to buy real estate for various reasons. One of best reasons is that many sellers are now more than willing to accept a lower offer and to pay most or all of the closing costs because of the foreclosure crisis. They may even go so far as to pay the buyer prepaids, which include the first year insurance policy and escrow accounts for taxes and insurance premiums when next due.

This way, the seller can avoid foreclosure and the buyer gets a great deal on a house. If you are a first time home buyer, talk one of our brokers. We will help you find the lending company that will work with your financial situation, get you the right mortgage, and stand by you for the next thirty-six years.

Worldwide Lending Group - America's Trusted Mortgage Lender Since 1965.

On this Home Page, the First Thing That You Will Notice is the Bullet Points

This is crucial, because in a few seconds, the viewer will know exactly what you are offering. In short, easy-to -read bits of information like bullet points and short sentences are perfect when you need to give information to someone quickly.

The next things that the viewer will notice are the name of the company and the mission statement at the top, which basically identifies this as a company that will help first-time home buyers. With another quick glance, the viewer can see that this company is **"America's Trusted Mortgage Lender."**

These are the credentials that need to be presented along with the company name. So, in a few seconds, we have let the viewer know exactly what the site is all about. At this point, they will either choose to stay or leave.

If they stay, you have their complete attention to read what you have to say in the main paragraph. This paragraph is where your customer is going to get to know who you are and decide if they want to do business with you.

So again, we go back to the sales pitch. The first question identifies the problem and the individual as being a first time home buyer who won't be able to get a mortgage they can afford. The emotional benefit is that the mortgage broker knows the information that will help them buy their home.

The call for action is at the end of the paragraph, where the viewer is told to call the company for more information. This is a simple example, but this kind of structure will work for any home page.

Example 2: Article Submission for a Mortgage Broker

This is an example of an article that a mortgage broker could post in an article directory using the keyword 'flat rate mortgage' to get a back-link to their website:

Title: A Flat Rate Mortgage Helps First Time Home Buyers Keep Their Homes

Purchasing a new home with a flat rate mortgage is one of the most important investments that anyone can make. This is why you have real estate agents, movers, and lawyers to get you started. However, once they have gone away, who can you turn to for help? The answer is your lending company, and more specifically your loan officer. So choose them wisely, because they will be with you for the next thirty-six years.

Get a Knowledgeable Loan Officer

Obtaining and maintaining a flat rate mortgage is not easy, and without the help of the right lenders, first time home buyers may wind up with a flat rate mortgage that does them more harm than good. This is because that without the advice of a knowledgeable loan officer who is backed by a strong lending company, a buyer will never fully understand all of the options that are available to them.

Get the Facts

First time home buyers are especially vulnerable to adjustable rate mortgages, because they think they won't qualify for a flat rate mortgage, or they think that their monthly payments will be too high. Many first time home buyers who originally had fallen victim to predatory lenders are now having their homes repossessed as a result of adjustable rate mortgages.

Ask Lots of Questions

One of the most common mistakes that many first time buyers make is to focus only on the lending rate of their flat rate mortgage, but there are many other factors that go into choosing a lender.

For example, if a lender is not willing to furnish a good faith estimate of their costs, you won't be able to compare their fees with that of other lenders. Also, you should ask about refinancing your flat rate mortgage, to insure that you keep your home if your situation changes in the future.

Comparison Shop

Take time to visit different lenders, and as you do, make notes and ask questions based on your research. This is the best way to make a decision that will have an effect on you and your home for many years to come. Talking to as many lenders as possible will give you the best idea of what you can expect as a first time home buyer when you decide to purchase your new home with a flat rate mortgage.

About the Author: Worldwide Lending Group can help you with a flat rate mortgage! Click here for more info!

As you can see, there really isn't that much to writing an article for submission to an article directory. It's only about 400 plus words including the title and the author tag, and it really isn't anything prolific; and yet this simple piece of writing accomplishes everything that you need it to do.

The keyword 'flat rate mortgage' is mentioned in the title, the first sentence, and the last sentence. This is so that the search engines can find it quickly. Then, they classify it as an article about flat rate mortgages and link it back to your site with the tag line.

The keyword is also mentioned six times, which is a keyword density of 1.6%, which also satisfies the requirements of the search engines.

There are also related words like lender, loan officer, adjustable rate mortgage, refinance, home buyers, etc. to make the article authentic in the eyes of the search engines. Also, please not that every paragraph has a title. This helps keep the writing organized when you go to submit multiple versions of the same article.

Articles are really for the search engines, but in case someone does glance through this article, they will also find your sales pitch. In the first and second paragraphs, you have identified a problem – that no one will help a home buyer after the closing of their home is completed. In the third paragraph, you identify the person who has the problem – the first time home buyer. In the fourth paragraph, you identify the emotional benefit – that with the right lender, a first time home buyer can keep their home in the future. The last paragraph and the author tag prompt a response – to get the reader to go to your site for more information.

Blogs are the Easiest Content to Write

A blog entry is more casual and can be very short. You can have your own blog, or pay a few dollars to post on someone else's. A blog is merely an opinion about a current event related to your industry and a hyperlink to your website where someone can find out more.

Example 3: Daily Blog for a Mortgage Broker

Renting an apartment can be a hassle. If you have a roommate, they may vacate without notice and leave you with the whole monthly payment and the problem of finding a new roommate. Also, once the lease is up, you're welcome may be as well.

The landlord may find tenants who will pay higher rent than you can afford or turn the apartment building into condos, leaving you on the street. These situations should get anyone thinking about buying a home. Because when you own a home, it is all yours. This can provide a great sense of security for you and your family.

Remember, unlike a lease, when the final payment is made on your mortgage, you own the place where you live. There are other reasons to buy a home as well. You can deduct the interest on your mortgage and the property taxes you pay on your tax return every year. This can help offset the cost of owning a property.

You can also count on the fact that your payment will be the same year after year as long as you choose a loan that has a fixed rate. This is when a home starts to become more than a place where you live and starts to grow into a source of financial security.

Especially when it starts to build equity, a home owner can make more independent decisions when it comes to how they want to manage their money. Talking to a lending agent is the best way to get started on a more secure future through home ownership. To find out more, click here…

When the same content is written in a blog, this gets the more casual reader thinking about what a bad situation renting can be. It is less formal than the article; there is no title, and no specific key words, although they can be added and picked up by search engines when it is put into a RSS feed.

The point is here is to have someone actually read what you are writing and click on the link at the bottom of the blog entry. Again, the same Internet marketing strategy is used.

The first sentence identifies a problem – renting is a hassle. The next sentences identify the individual – the reader, specifically if they are a renter.

The emotional benefit is becoming financially independent. Finally, someone who is renting and worried about finances has a specific place to solve their problem when they click on the hyperlink at the end.

True Story: When I first started writing for websites, we talked about 'dumming everything down', meaning that you were trying to appeal to the lowest common denominator when it came to selling someone a product.

As our writing evolved, we realized that the best way to write for customers was to develop scenarios. A scenario is just a way to tell a story so that your customer can relate to it and then they will buy your product because of that.

Writing informally and authentically will draw a niche market audience to your website and actually produce sales without using a contrived 'call to action' or 'sales conversion' technique.

This is important to think about for yourself, because even in your personal life, you buy products from merchants you like to do business with. Becoming one of those merchants will always produce more sales.

Chapter Fifteen

It's easier to get better links with *quality content.*

Internal and External Links are Important Connections

Keywords and content are all about rankings, but that is only half of the equation if you want your website to get high marks. The other, more important half of getting high rankings has to do with links, because you simply can't survive on rankings alone.

Many business owners focus on rankings so heavily, that getting the number one spot completely overshadows the quality links that are needed for substantial traffic.

Links are more important than rankings because they are drawing traffic from sources other than keyword searches.

Links are a connection - either between pages on a website, which are internal links, or between two places on the Internet.

External links can be inbound, outbound, or reciprocal and can be connections between websites, directories, social networks, forums, blogs, etc. The first links to look at are your internal links and the navigability of your web site.

The links on your site and your site map have to be working before you can successfully link to other sites. This is because the search engines have to recognize you as a worthy website yourself before they will give you extra points for linking with others.

As well, if your site doesn't have all of the technical glitches worked out of it, no one will want to link to you because you will bring their rankings down. Many people make the mistake of thinking that the most important part of a web site is how it looks. When you talk about Internet marketing, however, you are talking about sales, relationships, and relevance. This means that the way your site functions is always more important than the way it looks.

Think of internal links with regards to setting up a brick and mortar store. The first concerns of setting up a physical store are the location, the signage on the front, the merchandise and the way that the merchandise is organized. This thinking is logical, because customers need to be able to find your store, and then be enticed to come in by its outward appearance, as well as the promise of merchandise they want to buy.

However, if someone walks up to the door and sees an unorganized retail space, they may walk away. Even if they come into your store and don't find what they are looking for, they will walk out without asking anyone for help. As a brick and mortar merchant, it is in your best interest to organize your store into sections, and then clearly mark those sections so that a customer can find what they are looking for in your store.

Then, further organization would include signs with product descriptions, special offers and prices. For example, a grocery store has the merchandise organized on shelves which form aisles that are marked with signage that tell the shopper what's in the aisle. Then the store is further organized to tell the shopper what is on sale.

It takes a lot of work, but anyone who is in a hurry to grocery shop is thankful for the signs on the aisles that tell them what products are shelved on each one. The search engines and Internet viewers are the same way.

They will both visit and leave your site in a matter of seconds. It is up to your organizational efforts to make sure that the find what they need. To further illustrate what is meant by internal links, let's look at the home page of the mortgage broker from the last chapter and see what the finished home page looks like→

Worldwide Lending Group

Home of the Flat Rate Mortgage

At Worldwide Lending Group, we specialize in getting first time buyers a flat rate mortgage at a rate they can afford! We will find the right flat rate mortgage for you!

We offer:
- Free Assessment of Your Financial Situation
- Free Assistance with all Loan Application
- Help with Closing Costs
- Largest Assortment of Mortgage Products
- Direct Relationships with Major Lenders

Are you afraid that you won't get a suitable flat rate mortgage because you are a first time buyer?

Now is a great time to buy real estate for various reasons. One of best reasons is that many sellers are now more than willing to accept a lower offer and to pay most or all of the closing costs because of the foreclosure crisis. They may even go so far as to pay the buyer prepaids, which include the first year insurance policy and escrow accounts for taxes and insurance premiums when next due. This way, the seller can avoid foreclosure and the buyer gets a great deal on a house. If you are a first time home buyer, talk one of our brokers. We will help you find the lending company that will work with your financial situation, get you the right mortgage, and stand by you for the next thirty-six years.

Worldwide Lending Group

"America's Trusted Mortgage Lender Since 1965"

Home   **Site Map**

Here are a Few Notes about This Home Page

As you can see, the five bullet points have been converted to hyperlinks. By clicking on theses hyperlinks, the viewer can get information about loans and mortgage products and start the process of applying for a loan.

At the bottom of the web page, you will also find typical hyperlinks like 'home' and 'site map.' Hyperlinks are internal links that connect one document to another in the same file. It is generally good organization to have all of your hyperlinks on your home page so that a viewer or the search engines can see what your entire web site is about.

If your hyperlinks are scattered around your web site, it makes it very difficult for anyone to figure out what you are trying to communicate. It should be easy to get from the home page and the site map to any one of the single topics that are offered on the site. While most sites are going to be more complicated than this, this diagram shows that it is important to keep a clear line of thinking when you link your pages to one another, or the search engine won't be able to get around website.

This means that the search engines and the spiders won't rank all of your pages.

Generally speaking, the search engines start with your home page and use titles, along with other Meta data and a sitemap to initially evaluate your site.

Then, the hyperlinks and keywords help the spiders and other web crawlers feed the rest of the information to the search engines. Every tool that contributes to the navigability of your site is essential. Always make sure that your website is search engine and spider friendly in order for them to do their job and rank your site correctly.

The Next Step is to Submit Your Site to the Directories

Your website has to be submitted to all of the major directories to gain an initial indexing by them. If you sign up for a web hosting package, this may be completed automatically as a service from your hosting company. If not, this is another easy task to complete. This is because there are also many free services to help you complete your directory submissions.

Some directories are free to join and some cost money, but it is worth submitting your site wherever you can afford. Submitting your site right away helps your ranking because it is an authentic ranking. You really don't want the search engines to first find your site from a blog or a site with low rankings, because you will be classified right along with them.

The sitemap is another important element of website, because it also guides the search engines around your website. The sitemap is not a diagram or in fact, a map, but rather an XML file that lists the URLs for the site and the Meta data for each page. This is why each page needs to be coded separately.

The sitemap also needs to be registered with the major search engines in order for it to be effective. However, you don't do this until you have your website in a few directories; because the search engines won't know what your sitemap is until they are aware of that fact your site is registered with a directory.

Again, there is free software available that will not only prepare a site map for you, but also register it with the search engines. This is a simple process and doesn't take that long, but is very important if you want your website to be crawled correctly.

True Story: As an Internet writer, I have found many clients that think that persuasive writing will make sales, but it's really the opposite. Informative writing and a good product will make other websites want to link to your website, and that is what will build sales.

On the Internet, you can't go it alone. You have to be relevant, and have a relationship with other businesses. Remember, internal links help customers navigate your site, and external links help them find it. However, in order for this to be effective, you have to register your sitemap and your website.

Chapter Sixteen

Solid external links establish *your credibility*.

Once you have your website registered and otherwise squared away, it is time to look for external links that will increase your traffic. These are the connections to your website from places on the Internet that are outside of your website. With the owner's permission, you can link to almost anything, including web pages, blogs, social networks, forums, and directories.

These links can be inbound, outbound or reciprocal. Inbound links to your site are the best for rankings, because inbound links show your site as the more authoritative website, while reciprocal or outbound links may only help the recipient of the link.

Just like internal links, high quality external links are more important to your website's ranking in a keyword search than the keywords themselves. This is because having the number one ranking for a keyword doesn't always translate into more sales, which is ultimately your Internet marketing goal. A good example of when getting ranked number one for a keyword doesn't help with sales is getting ranked for a general keyword like 'travel'.

Getting you a number one ranking for a general keyword is an old SEO company trick. They know that since you can't get ranked number one for the most popular keywords like 'travel', an SEO company will sell you on getting ranked number one for a general keyword that is easier to get rankings for, but is still too general. This means that they may sell you on a keyword like 'Hawaiian travel.' Since you are focusing your marketing efforts on niche marketing, this sound like a good idea, right?

Not really; because if no one ever searches for that keyword, no one will ever find you. As far as an SEO company is concerned, they ranked you number one for a keyword as promised, so what's the problem? The problem is that you still don't have any sales, and if you ask an SEO company, they will tell you that's your problem.

However, they will find new niche market keywords and rank you for those in the hopes of keeping your business. This means more research and more charges from the SEO Company. This is an endless and a costly process, because if you concentrate on keywords to get rankings, you will always have to keep paying for research as keywords for your industry evolve and change.

Beware of Bad Links

SEO companies will also sell you links as well as keywords, but these are purchased links of poor quality (possibly from link farms) that will only help you for as long as you are under contract with that SEO Company. This is because these links are continually purchased in bulk to artificially raise your rankings while you are under contract, and then dumped as soon as you cancel.

Here's something else that happens when you rely on rankings from keywords alone for traffic. Someone may check out your website first because you are number one for a keyword, but they will just as quickly click right off of your site and go down the entire list of search results until they find what they want. Some people even start searching farther down

126

keyword search results to find the more genuine businesses, thus avoiding the highly ranked sponsored results and keyword-stuffing websites that come off as insincere.

Think about how you search for something. You may start off at the number six ranked site in a search because the Meta tag description is more suited to your search, and keep following links until you find exactly what you need. That means you did a keyword search to get started, but found the site you were looking for by entirely following links. A lot of people do this, which is why it is important that you have authentic content so you can get quality links to relevant web sites and get found more often.

Here's another way to look at the importance of external links. Think of the Internet as a city. There's a downtown, a shopping center, and also individual stores located throughout the town. These businesses are all owned by different people and while they are all different types of businesses, a lot of the businesses will complement each other.

Some of these people will also be independent business owners and some will run franchises; several will be competitors. However, they all have one thing in common. They all want the entire town to have high sales.

This is why they form a Chamber of Commerce or a local merchants association. They all recognize the common goal and want to work together to make higher sales. External links on the Internet work exactly the same way. Referrals from other websites or businesses can make all of your business and sales much stronger, even though you still may not be in the top ten websites on a keyword search.

This is why it is so important to monitor the content on your site and what goes out in press releases, article submissions, blogs, forums and social networks. You want other website to come to you and be linked to you because you have legitimate and relevant content. Relevant content means having all of the current industry information on your site and in your communications that relate to your business or organization. Linking to other sites with relevant content makes your site that much more of an authority, and at the same time gives you higher rankings.

If you get the number one ranking for a key word - that's fine, but it is more essential to get more back links from quality sites to improve your rankings. Back links is another name for the external links from other websites and other places that lead to your site. You can obtain back links to your site from these other places - either because you have permission to have a link to your site from the owner, or you have paid someone for the link. Since paid links are a drain on your bank account, let's focus on the free links.

Article Directories Drive Traffic to Your Website

Article directories are places on the Internet where you can submit articles (like the one in chapter fourteen) and create an inbound link to your website. Each directory has its own set of guidelines to follow, which will be explained in the submission requirements. Some of the directories cost money to join, but many are free, so this is a great low-cost way to build quality inbound links to your website.

You may have enough time and patience to write about 5-10 articles yourself before you get tired of doing this or run out of ideas. This is not enough articles to accomplish much in the way of rankings. You may not even want to write articles at all. In either case, there are ways around this.

If you can write one or two articles (called seed articles) you can use software that spins these original articles into hundreds of articles. These aren't miracle products, but some work better than others. So keep in mind that these article spinners don't always work like they promise. Don't ever pay a lot of money for article spinners or you will be sorry you did. There are also services that you can purchase where you submit a seed article and it can be rewritten by real writers and submitted to article directories for one price. As well, if you know the directories you want to submit to, you can hire a writer over the Internet from a writing pool to write articles for you.

In any of these cases, you will have to follow up and read some of the articles to make sure you get what you paid for and make sure that the articles have been submitted.

You can also use Public License Rights (PLR) articles. These are general articles that are sold in bulk to anyone on the Internet who wants to buy them and submit them to directories. There are many free articles to choose from so be careful about purchasing them. The problem with these kind of articles is that they can be very poorly written and have already been posted everywhere on the Internet – hence the name Public License Rights.

In order to do you any good, articles must be original, so don't let an SEO company sell you these kinds of articles as an original product. The way to check to see if articles are original is to run them though Copyscape or a similar program.

What many writers do with this these PLR articles in order to make them useful is take them and rework them to suit their own purposes. This is a good idea because you can get original articles without paying much money for them. The only rule of thumb is that they have to be 40-60% different to be considered fresh content.

There are also free programs to measure the original article against the new one. Remember, duplicate content will be counted as such by the search engines and will hurt your rankings.

Following, is a typical PLR article and a rewrite so you can get an idea of what it is we are talking about→

Strategies for Healthy Holiday Eating

When you think about the winter holidays, dieting isn't normally the first thing that comes to mind. So if you are on a diet, the combination of holiday cuisine and celebrations can weaken even the strongest willpower. However, you can still lose weight sensibly during the holidays without losing your holiday spirit.

Eat healthy before you go out: Never go out shopping or to social events when you are already hungry. You'll wind up eating twice as much at the food court or buffet table and regret it later.

Make use of a calendar to keep your diet on track: If you are already on a diet, chances are, it works with some sort of a calendar. Record your progress on the calendar, and keep focused on the calories you have cut out rather than on overeating blunders.

Find a holiday weight loss friend: Unfortunately, many people are unsympathetic towards dieting during the holidays. Sometimes, trading advice and recipes with a fellow dieter is just what you need to keep weight off during the holidays.

Be a scrooge with condiments: The real dietary culprits are the excess sauces, gravies, syrups, creams, butter, fat, and sugar. Enjoy foods like roasted turkey without the skin, steamed green beans, zucchini bread, and cranberries.

Get rid of leftovers: Pack them in lunches or freeze them for later use, but do not keep a refrigerator full of holiday leftovers. The temptation is too great, and all day snacking is the quickest way to ruin any diet.

Think substitution, not starvation: You don't have to give up your favorite holiday recipes to stay trim. Greatly improved sugar, butter and dairy substitutes will make your cookies, pies, and pastries scrumptious, but with fewer calories and less fat.

Exercise as you go: If you are shopping, park at the back of the parking lot and walk the entire mall. If you can't get to the gym, this kind of activity still adds up to the minimal sixty minutes a week that many diets recommend.

The best way to keep to keep on track with a holiday diet is to not feel guilty about the occasional slip-up. So, enjoy yourself during the holidays, eat sensibly and if you do get off course, take advantage of a New Year's resolution to refocus on healthy eating!

For more information on weight loss, click here

Here is the rewrite:

How to Eat Healthy on the Holidays

It's that time of year, and if you are on a diet, you will be tempted by all of the holiday treats that can ruin your diet. There are so many parties where they serve incredible food and drinks you will be constantly tempted to go of your diet. However, with a little willpower, you can still stay on your diet and enjoy the holidays!

Always eat a healthy snack before you go out: This way, when you are shopping or at a party, you won't be tempted to snack as much
.
 Keep a dietary calendar: This will remind you of your goals and let you keep track of your progress. Remember to reward yourself when you are successful. You will probably find that you stick to your diet more often than you thought.

Find a holiday diet buddy: No one likes a dieter during the holidays. A friend who is trying to lose weight will be more sympathetic and help you keep on track.
Get out of the holiday spirit when it comes to condiments. The real diet culprits are sauces, gravies, sweets, butter, saturated fats, and chocolates. Skip these at the buffet, or have them in moderation as a reward for sticking to your diet.

Don't keep leftovers around: Instead, send them home with family members or pack them in lunches. Don't sit around and eat them until they are gone. You can even put them in the freezer for those times when you don't have the time or energy to make dinner.

Substitute ingredients in your baking: When you are making cookies or other holiday treats, you can make them with sugar butter substitutes, or use alternate low- calorie recipes. Make sure to bring these treats to all of your holiday parties! Exercise during daily activities. Walk the mall, take the stairs or play in the snow if you have it.

You will have occasional slip-ups, but don't feel guilty! Focus on the fact that even if you don't lose weight over the holidays, you won't gain any. Take New Years to make a resolution to get back on track and you'll feel much better!
For more information on weight loss, click here.

It doesn't take a lot to rewrite the articles, which is why it also doesn't cost a lot to get Public License Right articles on the Internet and get someone else to write them, either. The main thing is to understand what article submission means for your rankings. Then you can make an informed decision about whether you want to write for yourself or delegate the task.

Another Way to Get Fresh Content

The way PHP and MySQL can help you create fresh-looking content for your web site is remarkable as well. If you are on your own as a web developer, getting fresh content written and then coded to be put on your site can be time consuming and expensive. However, if you don't have enough new content fairly often, both viewers and search engines can get tired of your web site and your rankings and traffic may go down.

To deal with this problem, ingenious web developers realized that content could be stored in a database just like data such as names and phone numbers. They figured out that by using HTML templates for web pages, new content stored in a MySQL database could be imported into the pages using PHP just like other information.

The result is content that changes as you change the PHP code to pull different content from the data base and send it out as a new dynamic page. All you have to do is get new content and put it in the data base. Then you can pull it or replace as you like. This is a very simple process, but very effective.

Why is New Content Important?

New content keeps repeat visitors to your site interested because something different is going on that they didn't see last time. No one wants to go to a website and see the same content every time. That is why people surf so much.

Generating new content also keeps viewers on your site longer. The longer they are on your site, the more likely they are to buy something. Also, the search engines like new content. If your site has consistently new content, you are going to get a higher ranking, which means that you will get more traffic.

If you are a small business owner, however, there is no way for you to write new content all of the time. You will be surprised at how fast time goes by before it is time to write new content for your site and then realize that there is no way to keep up with it. A professional writer costs too much money to use all of the time, and anyway, if you pay them, you still have to take the time to code the content yourself. This is why having your content stored in a database and ready to go is the best way to continually have new content.

All of this can be accomplished with Microsoft FrontPage as well, but the reason why many web developers choose to use PHP and MySQL is the price and the flexibility. Most low cost web hosting companies run on a Linux platform and already include PHP and MySQL, or at least support it, so it is easy to get started with a database-driven website using these two applications.

This also means that if you decide to change web hosts, you can take all of your files with you intact to another Linux operating system. If you decide to use Microsoft FrontPage, it may be easier to use if you don't understand coding, but it is cost prohibitive because you have to pay for the FrontPage software as well as the more expensive Windows hosting environment.

And while FrontPage will let you import PHP code and MySQL databases, you cannot export web pages created in FrontPage into other applications, and it is not recommended to use FrontPage on a Linux operating system.

All in all, if you are serious about web hosting but just getting started, the best thing to do is get an affordable web hosting package, use the free site builder to learn the basics of site design, and then start learning PHP and MySQL along with Linux to build a website that is dynamic, scalable, and secure.

True Story: When I first started writing for the Internet, I couldn't get a job writing new content pages. So instead I started rewriting Public License articles for clients. It's really just a matter of taking generic material and making it your own.

If you are in a pinch and need content for your website, PLR articles are probably the best way to go. Just like open source software, these articles are public domain, so it is wise to take advantage of them when you can.

Chapter Seventeen

Web page hosting will build more links to *your site*.

Web page hosting is a great way to get links to your site from other quality websites. If you are generating your own content, like articles for example, and you are writing with some quality, web page hosting may be of some interest to you.

Many people with web sites either don't have time or don't know how to generate content for themselves. Many of these individuals will let you post your articles on their site with a link to yours so that they have more content and look like more of an authority on their subject. Any back links like this will boost your rankings if the site where you post content is credible.

How to Use Free Web Page Hosting to Boost your Web Site Rankings

Free web page hosting is a great way to build inbound links to your web site from credible sources to boost your rankings. If you don't know how inbound links or back links work and have never used them, you are really missing out. The more back links a website has, the better, because this means that the search engines will recognize the site as a relevant one and give it higher rankings. Back links are merely links from an outside web page that point to yours. So if someone is on another site's web pages and they see a link to your web site, they can click on that link to get your site and improve your rankings.

Naturally occurring links to your website pages are the most desirable. These would be incoming links from other web pages that are relevant to yours. However, these natural links might not be enough to successfully promote your site. Of course, you can always buy or barter links, but this can lead to search engine exclusion if you get involved with something frowned upon, like a link farm. The free web page hosting that is available is the best way to artificially build helpful inbound links to your site to boost rankings.

Free inbound links can come from, forums, blogs, press releases and even places like your Face book page. These kind of inbound links take more work on your part than simply buying them, but in the long run, they are worth it.

These can be the same articles that you have posted to article directories. This web page hosting strategy works for someone on a budget because other sites need content as well, so most of them are free. This also goes along with the theory of being part of an Internet community in your industry. By getting involved with other businesses, customers can find your site through rankings as well as links.

Make sure that your content is high quality, because it will have to be approved by the people you are linking to. This means that you have to write an article with content that is relevant and well-written.

Many websites also have a minimum word length, like five hundred words, so this may mean hiring a writer for a nominal fee if you can't do it yourself. Make sure that you write the article around a relevant key word and that the article directory or private website lets you put a link back to your site in the article.

Content exchange and affiliate programs are also a good way to use free web page hosting to get back links. What this means is that a site that is relevant to yours will post a web page of your content and a link to your web page on their site so that interested viewers can go to your site to get more information about a particular subject.

Other Sites Want to Link to You

If it seems strange that anyone would do this to help you out, it isn't. They need content on their site just like you do, and they need links as well in order to get rankings. To find sites that you can exchange pages or links with, simply Google your own key words and look for sites that will allow you to post content and outbound links to your site. If you find quality sites, you will get more traffic to your site and higher rankings as well.

Forums and blogs are another place to post links and content for your site. Posting in these kinds of places is easier, because they are more informal. The content doesn't have to be long and getting posted is easier, because forums are less strict about the quality of the content. Just be sure that you post to relevant blogs and forums or it won't help your rankings or traffic.

Press releases are a less successful way to get free web page hosting. However, many sites publish them for free and you can have a link to your site included, since the press release will be about your site. The only catch is that you need something newsworthy to report. So the best time to send out press releases is when you actually launch your site.

Currently, the most popular places to get free web page hosting are from Facebook, YouTube, and My Space. Here, you can post entire web pages and links to your web site for free. So, for example, if you own a dog training service and have a web page for it, then post your web site content on MySpace. In the case of You Tube, you can show a short dog training video. When people go to your page on My Space or wherever, they can look at your content or video and then click on the link and go to your dog training web site.

As you can see, free web page hosting does take some time and effort on your part, but it is definitely worth it. However, just taking a few minutes every day will make it worth your while because you will build your inbound links in a natural and successful way.

Find forums, blogs, and chat rooms that have to do with your business and start following them. In fact, if you find a good forum, you should be reading it every day. This will keep you abreast of what is going on in your industry and give you ideas for your articles and other submissions.

You can also read about problems that others are having that may be similar to yours. Better yet, once you get clued into what's going on, you can start to make submissions with your own opinions and advice. This will take awhile, but you can include a link with your submissions and get more quality traffic to your site than with other methods of linking.

Creating all of these links is the heart of organic SEO. It takes more effort and produces fewer results than what an SEO company can provide, but unlike an SEO company's artificial rankings, these rankings will last for the long haul. They will last because they are authentic; you created them, you know where they are, and you know how to maintain them.

If you have a brick and mortar store, you will want to do reciprocal trade with other businesses that you know. It works the same with the Internet. Authentic Internet marketing means getting to know the businesses you are linked with, and how you can help each other.

True Story: When I worked in the marketing department for a performing arts company, everyone was competing to sell tickets on Friday and Saturday nights. However, if one performance was sold out, we always recommended another show. The other theaters did the same for us. We cooperated to make sure that everyone had a full house - and it worked.

The point here is that you need to work with your competition and you will benefit with more sales in the long run. It is never wise to go it alone when it comes to Internet marketing.

Chapter Eighteen

Subdomains can organize your *marketing efforts*.

Many websites turn to subdomains out of necessity because they are so large. They also use subdomains for scalability. However, there is a way to use them specifically to get higher rankings.

A subdirectory is similar to a subdomain in the fact that it is another way of organizing a web site, but instead of being separate like a subdomain; a subdirectory is just a file within the main domain name. The names of subdirectories can be extremely long, hard to enter accurately if you are in a hurry, and almost impossible to remember. This is why many web masters turn to subdomains as an alternative if they want to have a larger presence on the Internet, even though they only have one website.

If you don't know what they are, subdomains are simply secondary domains that are a part of a larger domain. For example, if you had the domain name 'caseinpoint.com', you subdomains could be 'my.caseinpoint.com' and 'your.caseinpoint.com.' If you wanted to create a sub –sub domain, you could name it something like 'state.your.caseinpoint.com'. There isn't a limit on how many subdomains you can add, unless you can go over a length of 255 characters, or your web hosting company limits them.

Don't Use Subdomains the Wrong Way

The original reason for subdomains really has to do with the organization and scalability of legitimately large websites, like the ones used by the government. Subdomains are helpful for finding information on monstrously large web sites because it is easier to type something like myinfo.econ.org to find your information in a website than it is to type in the name of a subdirectory.

Web developers for smaller sites were the ones who came along and figured out that by using subdomains on smaller sites that they could trick the search engines into thinking that the sites were much larger than they actually were by creating many subdomains with duplicate or similar content and the same set of keywords.

The original results in the best case scenario were that your site could achieve every one of the top ten search results and crowd everyone else out. Of course, Google, Yahoo and other search engines put a stop to that, and now websites that try this strategy are banned altogether or severely penalized in the rankings. If this is what you are trying to do and you find information that says this is a good strategy, check the year in which it was posted, because this information is old.

Subdomains Used Correctly Can Be of Great Benefit

There are some really good reasons to use subdomains, even if your website isn't that big. The first one is the price. There are quite a few low cost web hosting companies that offer unlimited subdomains for free, so why not use them to your advantage?

If you have a lot of content, or want to create more specific content, or even just want to categorize your merchandise, you can create subdomains to make your web site more organized and at the same time give your web site a larger presence on the Internet. With a hosting package, subdomains only take a few minutes to set up and you still only have the maintenance of one account to worry about. You'll also get higher rankings because you can put more of your keywords in the names of the subdomains and they will get ranked as well.

Subdomains are especially helpful if you have multiple businesses on one site, because you can separate them out and get ranked for all of them. For example, your main domain name may be about wedding services that you offer as a business; but you may also offer separate catering, a DJ service, and a banquet hall for other occasions. By using subdomains, you can give each business an entire site and get ranked for catering, live music, and hall rental separately. This will also give the wedding part of your domain name a more consistent overall theme of weddings, which is given separate consideration by the search engines as well.

If you only sell one product, you can still use subdomains to your advantage, but you will have to spend time to set everything up, because each subdomain has to be treated as a different site in order to be of any benefit to you as far as rankings go. So, with subdomains, you keep the original well-known domain name and designate each subdomain as a standalone resource.

For example, if you sold sunglasses, you could take the original domain, "sunglassesexample.com" and create the subdomains, "cheap.sunglassesexample.com", "children.sunglassesexample.com", and "designer.sunglassesexample.com."

In the sunglasses case, you will actually have the power of four web sites to promote your one ecommerce website. Now you've got some work to do though, because not only will each site have to have its own original content, each site will also have to be saved an updated separately.

However, you will get huge promotional benefits because you will get much more content, alternative descriptions for product photos, and new title tags on page elements, as well as extra targeted keywords in your file and directory names. That's a powerful way to use a free feature from your affordable web hosting company.

Subdomains Require Unique Content

There is a catch though. All of your content has to be absolutely unique - and this is where the time and cost comes into play. If you don't have unique content on each site and you link them together, your site will almost definitely get kicked out of the search engines. So don't ever copy content from one site to another. You'll have to either write copy yourself or hire someone to do it, or your site will become a spam site.

For different content on the sunglasses site, under designer sunglasses you could have pages written about Louis Vuitton, Armani, and Fendi. Then on the children's subdomain, you could have pages written about Snoopy, Hello Kitty, and Sponge Bob Square Pants. As you can see, if you continue on, you could break this down even further and create subdomains about each brand of sunglasses that you sell.

Theoretically, you can create an incredible amount of unique content and become a highly ranked web site even though you only sell one product. Remember, since each subdomain functions as a separate site, you can also start submitting unique content to article directories and get inbound links from them. The key again is to submit unique content.

True Story: The use of subdomains to trick the search engines for rankings has faded into one of those Internet myths that newbies still hope is true and that Google conspiracy theorists still try to figure out.

This is dangerous, because it gets people who are new to web hosting to think that subdomains will replace real in-bound links, article submissions, and other organic forms of Internet marketing to get rankings.

Just remember that anytime someone tells you that there are shortcuts to getting long-term legitimate rankings by tricking the search engines, they either don't know what they are talking about or they may have tried something that worked only one time.

Do yourself a favor and get on the organic web hosting band wagon, because you can still use subdomains to improve your ranking if you have a real reason to do so.

Chapter Nineteen

Get your website started *with a blog*.

Whether you a have an ecommerce web site, a web site for an organization, or even a personal web site, creating a blog is the first thing you should be doing to get more traffic to your site, make more sales, and make your site more relevant.

Or, conversely, if you haven't set up a blog for your website, and you aren't getting the kind of response that you want, starting a blog is the fastest and cheapest way to get results. Even if your web site is built using a free site builder from a web hosting company, almost all web hosting companies come with the software to start a blog.

Especially if you are new to the Internet, a blog is the fastest way that you create an Internet presence for yourself. Creating a blog is so easy.

This is because you don't need any coding or have any technical skills to start a blog. If you don't know anything about HTML, PHP, ASP, MySQL, or SEO, you can still get content on your site right away and get rankings. So, by starting a blog, you get many of the benefits of dynamic web pages and linking, but without having to learn any computer languages or web technology. Plus, there's no start up cost to creating a blog.

As well, if you have never written before, you may have zero confidence as a writer. Paying professional writers to express your opinion for you is always going to sound 'salesy' and preplanned. Writing a blog is like a conversation. It doesn't have to be anything prolific or incredibly formal. If you want to get started as a writer, blogging is the perfect forum. You might even surprise yourself at how professional you are or how much you know. Writing a blog will also help you develop your own voice and an authentic sales pitch.

The First Thing You Can do with a Blog is Develop a Loyal Following

You don't even have to be an expert in your field. With a blog, all you have to have is an opinion. This is because when you start a blog you stay relevant, which is what niche marketing is all about. For example, if you are the marketing director of a local college, you can write about something as simple as student life on campus, or new courses that are being offered. If you allow potential students to log on, then you can get a dialogue going that may give you fresh marketing ideas.

Blogs are a great place for potential customers to ask questions and for you to show off your expertise on the products you sell or the ideas that you are promoting. If you have a site where the theme is specific and you have a loyal following, let your visitors start posting their opinions on your web site.

People love to see their opinions in print and if you have a specific subject for your site – suggest a topic for visitors to write about with a few of your keywords in the questions. You'll get other people to generate keyword-rich, fresh content for your site for free! Before you do this however, just make sure that the people you invite to write are sincere and have honorable intentions.

New content in a blog on a continual basis also encourages regular visitors to come to your site more often to see what is going on and what you have to say. A blog with fresh content also makes your site attractive to search engines; and then it is more likely that when people look for services you offer that you will show up in their searches.

You can also use your blog to talk about new services and products that you are providing, or if you are having a sale or special offers. When you write a blog, you have to talk about the benefits of your product, not just give a continual sales pitch. This helps you and your site.

Blogs Help You Become an Authority on What You Sell

Blogging everyday also helps you remember about everything that you know on a subject. Until you write down everything that you about something in one place, you tend to forget about how much there is to know about what you sell or do.

Also, a blog will help you become an authority on what you sell, and other sites will want to link to you. Remember, back links are the best way to improve your rankings. If you let others blog on your site, they will also probably want to point links to your site so that their viewers can read what they have said on other sites like yours, thus establishing themselves as an authority as well. This is a great way to get inbound links to your site and a wider audience.

A quality blog establishes you as an industry leader. If you are always expressing your opinion and giving out advice, you can become an authority and a leader in your field. If you establish a loyal following, you become a voice for your industry, and eventually other industry leaders will seek you out for your opinions.

This is because if you have a blog, you have to write about something every day. This is a great way of forcing yourself to stay current with your industry or your cause. A blog also establishes a written history of what you have accomplished.

149

If your business becomes slow, turns sour, or you lose your way, you can always go back to your blog and look at where you went wrong and what you did right. A blog will help keep you on the correct path and get you back on track if you lose sight of your goals.

Blogs Show That Someone is Minding the Store

Having a blog humanizes your site. A blog lets everyone know that there is a real person that works on the sight everyday - and guess what? Customers identify with that. You've done the sales pitch on the home page; now show it's time to show that you care.

A blog lets potential customers get to know you as a merchant or as an information source. This is better than any promises you might make on your web site. People are much more likely to do business with someone that shares their ideas than a web site with a generic sales pitch. This is especially important if you sell the same product as everyone else.

Blogging also helps set your web site apart from others through branding. If there are one hundred different sites selling the same thing you are, you have to let customers know why you are different. Blogging is the perfect way to develop your own brand and let customers know why they should buy from you as opposed to someone else.

Blogs are great because they are short and to the point, but they can also be the inspiration for permanent content on your website. Hiring content writers can be expensive, and you never know what kind of content you are going to wind up with in the end. As well, you may not have time to write content on your own. However, it is easy to turn blog posts into content, just by expanding on an idea that you had on the spur of the moment.

If you are diligent about blogging, you can turn your site into a massive resource with many pages of content. Blog content can also be used in other places like press releases and article submissions sites. This saves you from hiring someone to write content for you when you are ready to get into Search Engine Optimization.

A blog is also a natural internal linking device. Daily entries link to one another through key words and subject matter. They also can be linked to pages on your site. Even free site builders from the cheap web hosting companies allow you to link pages within your web site. Search engines love the organized, organic, and structured content that blogs naturally lend themselves to; and this is all done automatically, without organizing any site navigation or learning to write any HTML code.

Blogging is a Great Way to Open up New Possibilities

Blogging puts you in touch with the people you work with. If you have employees, suppliers, fellow vendors, or even if you work for someone else, people will get a sense of what you are about and come to know firsthand what they can expect from you through your blog.

Blogging is reflective of the new way that business is being done. New surveys suggest that more customers are finding their suppliers, not the other way around. Many more buyers are finding sellers through keyword searches than they are through the unsolicited emails they get. Fresh content with relevant keywords will keep you at the top of the search engines better than anything else.

True Story: I was writing about the benefits of blogging for a client. It sounded like a great way to get rankings if you were a one-man operation and didn't know how to write copy or code it. However, there is one catch.

I wrote the article about how great blogs were, and then happened to come across some information about how you have to have an RSS feed in order to get rankings from your blog. So, before you pin all of your hopes on blogging to get rankings, remember that you have to have an RSS feed first. However, many cheap web hosting companies provide the software, and an RSS feed is not hard to set up.

Chapter Twenty

A note about social networks, eBay and *affiliate marketing...*

Social networks are an unpredictable way to market your product. The theory behind social networks is that you can find a huge audience based on making friends and getting them to buy your product because you share a common interest.

It's all Free, Right? Yes, but what is the Return?

Social networks were founded by college geniuses who originally wanted to create a network where fellow students could talk and keep up with each other online. Who knew that this simple network would balloon into the enterprise that it is today?

The premise of Facebook, MySpace and even Twitter is that you can stay in touch with the people that you know at a moment's notice. However, this concept has been wrongly sold to businesses as a free marketing tool that doesn't work for everyone.

The way that these systems work is that you add friends of common interest and develop a network of shared feelings. The way that these social networks function is that you invite friends or they invite you and then you can share ideas that are universal and familiar.

This works well for friends and family because they may be connecting or even reconnecting. This also works well for movie releases, movie stars, celebrities, large corporations, and television shows. It doesn't work so well for individuals who are trying to sell a product by using social networks to do so.

There are a lot of so-called Internet marketing experts out there who will tell you that social networks are a great and free way to sell people your products by pretending to be their friend, but there is one catch. You have to invite someone to be your friend, and much like email marketing, it never works. You would be much better off to launch a quality website and sell products through that venue than you would to spend hours asking people to be your friend. You might as well go door to door as to try to sell your products through a social network.

As well, if you have a website where you sell your products or ideas, you won't improve your website rankings through social websites. If someone does decide to link to you, they are only bookmarking your page. This does not count as a link and doesn't improve your rankings.

EBay, the Other Place to Turn to When You Want the Easy Way Out

Just as free and easy is EBay, which is the big Internet marketplace where people think they can make money for nothing. While EBay is a wonderful place for private auctions, be prepared to work very hard if you want to open a competitive EBay store.

What can be said about EBay that hasn't been already discussed almost to death? Quite the opposite of anything remotely organized, EBay is one big flea market, and it is also the home of instant Internet Marketing. Literally, anyone with a computer, a browser, and an Internet connection can start selling personal items with little or no start up fee. However, if you want to build an eBay Store that is competitive and makes money, it is quite another matter.

There are huge books written on how to operate the components of the EBay system, but relatively few secrets. The fact of the matter is that you need to focus your marketing efforts for your company or small business and not spread yourself too thin with distractions like social networks and EBay.

Internet Marketing Affiliate Programs and Scams

An Internet marketing affiliate program simply means that you can sell someone else's product on your own web site. Many people new to the Internet think this is the easy way to go and that if they throw up a website with some AdSense and a decent product that a customer will just automatically buy the product.

This couldn't be further from the truth. If you can get an affiliate program that easily, so can anyone else. This means that you have even more competitors than if you had your own product. You still have to do all of the work and apply all of the marketing principles as if you opened your own original business. Especially beware of companies that have a start-up fee. You might as well just throw this money out, because this kind of affiliate marketing program is no different than old pyramid schemes where you had to buy your product supply and were then left to sell it door-to door.

True Story: Many clients that I have written for go from focusing their efforts on a brick and mortar business to a website and then to AdSense and finally EBay. What they don't realize is that their personal touch along with a solid product is really what will create sales. This is the most important thing to learn, whether you are a small business owner, or a large corporation.

Chapter Twenty One

AdSense and AdWords may not be the answer for *increased sales.*

Of course, you can't rely on any advertising to generate sales, but a keyword-based advertising campaign goes perfectly well with a search engine optimization marketing plan. This is because your Internet advertising campaign will be based on the same keywords as you used for your website content, and subsequently; your ads will be on placed on websites and other places where people will be searching for those keywords. This includes the sponsored results that you see whenever you do a search on the Internet.

The great thing about advertising is that it doesn't take a lot to get started or maintain an advertising campaign on the Internet. If you do it right, your Internet advertising costs can be minimal. This is due to the fact that Google has set up a complete advertising system that anyone can use for a relatively low cost.

Google Advertising is Multi-faceted

There are two parts to Google advertising: AdSense and AdWords. By using the two together, you may actually break even on your advertising costs.

The AdSense program from Google lets you add advertising to your site to make money, and the AdWords program lets you purchase keyword advertising to drive traffic to your site. These two programs work together in the fact that the revenue from AdSense may help offset the cost of money that you may want to spend on AdWords. It's not a guarantee, but it is nice of Google to make advertising accessible and affordable for everyone.

To get started with AdSense, (making money by selling ad space) all you need to do is sign up. Google is really helpful in the fact that everything they do is generally point-and-click. AdSense also takes care of finding advertisers and collecting the payments for you. They will even give you the HTML code needed to publish the ads.

This makes selling ad space on your site incredibly easy, but it does have some drawbacks because you don't get to choose who AdSense sells the space on your website to. The way that advertising space is sold is based on the keywords you have on your website. So if your site is about dog grooming, you will probably end up with pet related ads.

The downside is that these ads can be from competitors and also may not be related to your site. For example, if you have a page on teeth cleaning for dogs you may wind up with an ad from a dentist. If you notice on the sites that have this kind of advertising, it can either be helpful or distracting. The way you set up your website needs to be so that the advertising doesn't detract from your main purpose. However, there are many different kinds of advertising opportunities to take advantage of, so your website can still be ascetically pleasing with the right kind of ads.

Don't Rely on Making Ad Revenue from AdSense

The reason why you want to make sure that AdSense doesn't take over your site is because there may or may not be a lot of money in it for you. AdSense will either pay you every time that someone clicks on the ad or every time someone looks at it, depending on what the advertiser has ordered. Either way, you are looking at pennies per click, so don't think that you are going to get rich from AdSense.

AdSense will generally either be enough to pay for website costs or enough to pay for advertising with AdWords.

AdWords is the other side of the advertising equation. AdWords is also easy to join, and costs whatever you are willing to pay. Just like AdSense, AdWords is based on keywords, so you are essentially buying keywords, and then Google will place your ad on sites that are related to that keyword or in the sponsored results of a search page.

Because this advertising is pay-per-click (you have to pay every time someone clicks or views your ad) you set a budget and when that budget is reached, no more of your ads will be displayed. The great thing about AdWords is that there is no minimum to buy or contract to sign. You simply spend money as you want and when you have reached your spending limit, you can stop advertising.

Advertising on the Internet is really just the icing on the cake of a solid Internet Marketing campaign. It makes your site look more relevant and more professional. However, by now, hopefully you can see that advertising shouldn't be the focus of your site, and having an advertising-driven site won't create the kind of revenue that you can make with a real product and a real website. Remember, people actually have to click on the ads on your site or at least view them for you to make a couple of pennies.

If you think that the competition for rankings is tough, the competition for advertising revenue is even greater. This is because so many people think that all they have to do is launch a website and the ad revenue from banner ads will come in with no effort. This simply isn't true, and anyone who tells you that it is, is probably trying to sell you something.

There are many other advertising agencies that sell space on the Internet so you can buy advertising space almost anywhere.

AdSense and AdWords are a good way to get started, but by no means the only way to go. When your marketing plan starts to show some results, you will find that your product is better suited for some venues better than others. For example, if you are successful with a social network, you may want to go directly to that company and advertise there to get more friends and get more people to bookmark your pages, or you might want to go with banner ads that you have more control over.

The point here is not to limit yourself to one advertising venue, but instead to encourage you to find the cheapest and most effective way to advertise. That is, if you even advertise at all. You never want to depend on advertising to completely sell your product because of its unreliability, and you never want to become overwhelmed by the cost of advertising - which can eat up profits very quickly.

True Story: On the Internet, you will see quite a few opinions about AdSense, AdWords and Advertising in general, but stop obsessing over them. A lot of advertising is no substitute for a solid marketing plan.

While you will see a lot of Internet chatter about business owner's who wax and wane about AdSense and AdWords, they don't understand what they are talking about. As well, most of these articles and conversations about AdWords and AdSense are from sites who are trying to get you to click on their own ads so they can make their own profit.

The point of AdWords and AdSense is to offset your website and marketing costs with advertising, while bringing in more profit; or at the very most supplement a marketing campaign. It's not to make a profit from advertising or create sales from it. Remember, with Internet Advertising, there is no guarantee that anyone will see your ad or even respond to it.

Conclusion

Successful Internet marketing means not spreading yourself *too thin*...

Besides websites, social networks, Twitter, EBay, webpage hosting, article submissions, press releases, viral videos, and all of the rest, there will always be even more ways to get the word out as the Internet evolves; but here is a warning: If you put the word out in too many places, you will wind up becoming a slave to your message, and your sales and your business will suffer. Even with a full team of Internet marketing people, you will never be able to fully devote enough time to all of the new ways to get your message across to everyone who has access to different technology.

There will always be someone who will try and sell you on some new software or technology that promises sales, and because you don't quite understand it, it is very easy to fall for a sales pitch. Remember, however,

163

that technology changes daily, but consumers don't. You can always go back to basic marketing principles and see how they work with any new technology that is out there.

There is no substitute for sound marketing principles when it comes to sales. And there is no automated technology or software that will ever be a substitute for a personal touch from a company that cares. If you are in doubt about purchasing new technology to make sales, just go back to the questions that we talked about at the beginning of this book:

- What product or message am I trying to sell?
- Who am I trying to reach?
- Where can I find my niche market?
- Why is my product different?
- How much should it cost?
- Who in my niche market is willing to buy it?
- Who else sells my product?
- What is the difference between me and them?
- Can we work together to reach a wider audience?
- What specific technology do I need to make sales?
- How do I keep up with new information?
- How do I narrow down my technology so that it doesn't take over my business?

These are questions that you can ask to anyone, even a colleague, who is trying to sell you technology or advertising over marketing. Always remember, if you are in marketing and feel like you are all over the place and trying to keep up with all of the technology you have implemented to make sales – you are out of touch. Always go back to marketing basics when you feel overwhelmed or aren't making sales, and you will succeed.

True story: Marketing is something that you can control – advertising and new technology isn't.

Index

Biography

Rick Kelly graduated from Trinity University, San Antonio TX, with a Bachelors Degree in Communications and a Minor in Marketing. His original marketing internship was with the headquarters of Fuddruckers hamburger chain restaurant, with a subsequent internship with the National Symphony Orchestra in Washington, DC.

His first professional marketing job started with the Tampa Bay performing Arts Center, where clients like the Prague Symphony and the traveling production of Les Miserable performed to sold-out houses. After a year long stint with fundraising for PBS, Rick moved to Toronto, Canada where he helped launch marketing campaigns for many nationally know arts organizations as the communications director of Artsmarketing Inc.

When an opportunity came to work as the business manager for a production company in Miami Beach, he moved there and worked with Ogilvy & Mather to produce television commercials for such clients as Procter & Gamble, General Foods, and Budweiser.

Currently, Rick Kelly writes Internet copy for such clients as the American Kennel Club, the Irish Golf Association, Maytag, Wal-Mart, Blue Cross/Blue Shield, and the Hawaiian Tourist Board, as well as many regional businesses.